LET'S MAKE COMICS!

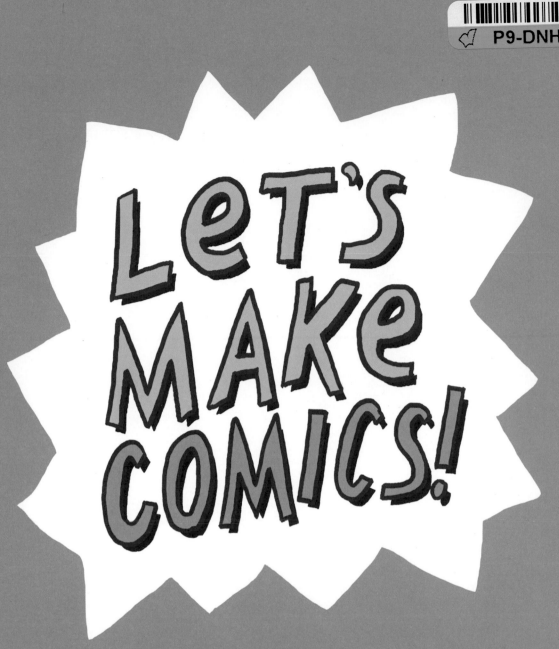

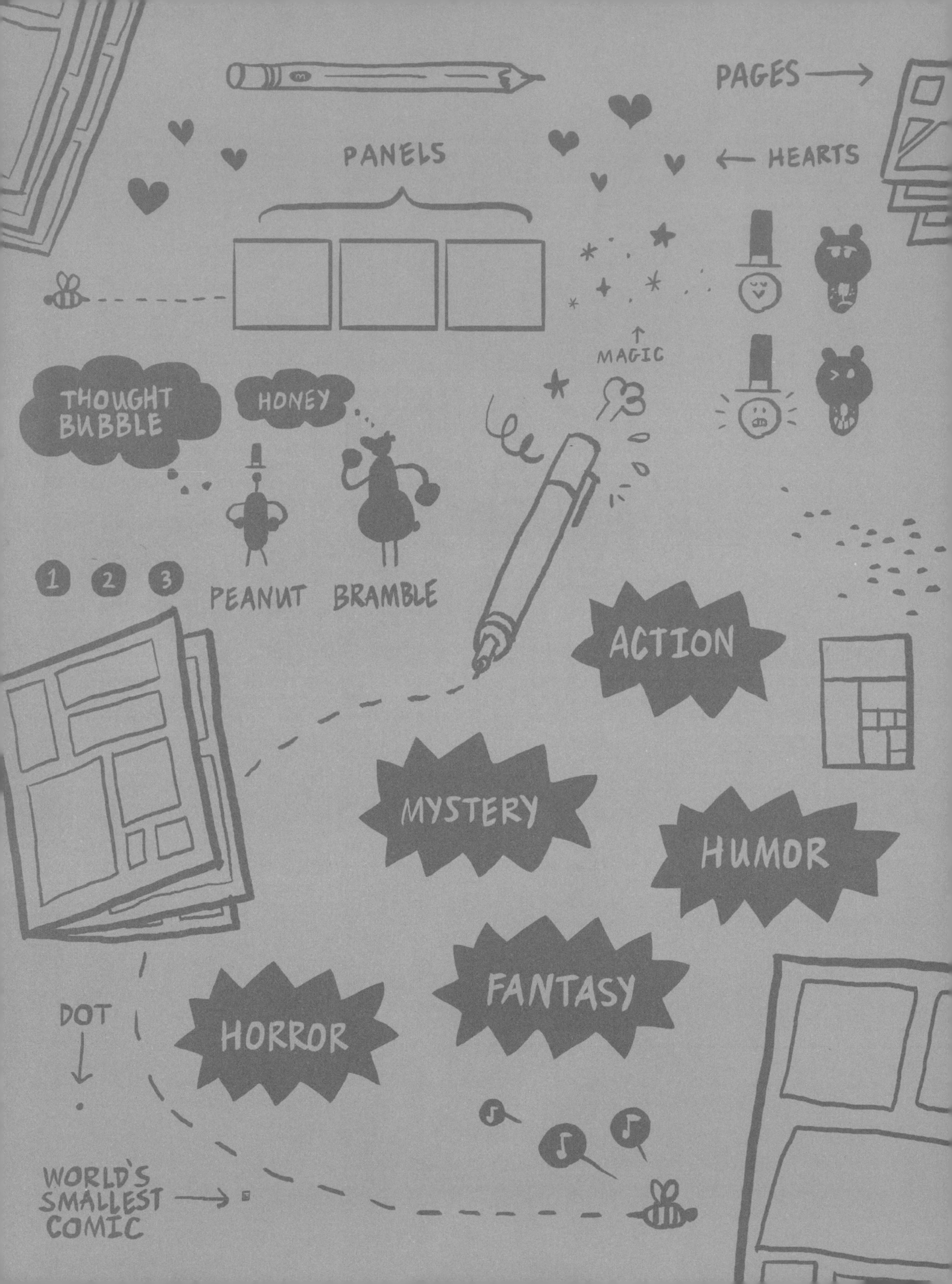
PAGES
PANELS
HEARTS
MAGIC
THOUGHT BUBBLE
HONEY
PEANUT
BRAMBLE
1
2
3
ACTION
MYSTERY
HUMOR
FANTASY
HORROR
DOT
WORLD'S SMALLEST COMIC

LET'S MAKE COMICS!

AN ACTIVITY BOOK TO CREATE, WRITE, AND DRAW YOUR OWN CARTOONS

JESS SMART SMILEY

WATSON·GUPTILL
CALIFORNIA | NEW YORK

THIS BOOK IS DEDICATED
TO MY FAMILY:
MIKELLE, NOAH, EVELYN, AND GRACE

Copyright © 2018 by Jess Smart Smiley

All rights reserved.
Published in the United States by Watson-Guptill Publications, an imprint of
the Crown Publishing Group, a division of Penguin Random House LLC, New York.
www.crownpublishing.com
www.watsonguptill.com

WATSON-GUPTILL and the HORSE HEAD colophon are registered trademarks
of Penguin Random House LLC

Library of Congress Cataloging-in-Publication Data
Names: Smiley, Jess Smart, author.
Title: Let's make comics! : an activity book to create, write, and draw your own
    artoons / Jess Smart Smiley.
Description: California : Watson-Guptill Publications, 2018. | Audience: Ages 7-10. |
    Audience: Grades 4 to 6. | Includes bibliographical references and index.
Identifiers: LCCN 2017058953
Subjects: LCSH: Comic books, strips, etc.--Technique--Juvenile literature. | Cartooning--
    Technique--Juvenile literature. | BISAC: ART / Techniques / Cartooning. | COMICS &
    GRAPHIC NOVELS / Nonfiction. | JUVENILE NONFICTION / Art / Cartooning.
Classification: LCC NC1764 .S59 2018 | DDC 741.5/1--dc23
LC record available at https://lccn.loc.gov/2017058953.

Trade Paperback ISBN: 978-0-399-58072-7

Printed in China

Design by Chloe Rawlins

10 9 8 7 6 5 4 3 2 1

First Edition

★ ★ ★ ★ CONTENTS ★ ★ ★ ★

INTRODUCTION

THIS BOOK IS PACKED WITH ACTIVITIES TO HELP YOU WRITE, DRAW, LETTER, AND INK YOUR OWN COMICS!

PEANUT!

SHOULDN'T WE MENTION **THE STARS** OF THE BOOK?

HERE'S HOW THE BOOK WORKS.

EACH ACTIVITY HAS A TITLE AND SOME DIRECTIONS.

...LIKE THIS!

TITLE
DIRECTIONS

THE COMIC GOES IN THE MIDDLE.

THE COMICS ARE MY FAVORITE PART.

I HEARD THERE'S A BEAR IN THESE COMICS...

YOU WILL FIND COMICS-MAKING SKILLS AND BONUS ACTIVITIES AT THE BOTTOM OF EACH PAGE!

...A VERY FAMOUS BEAR!

IT'S ME--BRAMBLE! I'M THE BEAR IN THESE COMICS!

READY? LET'S TRY ONE!

ACTIVITIES

WHAT'S BEHIND THE DOOR?

DRAW WHAT IS BEHIND THE DOOR IN EACH OF THE COMICS BELOW.

COMICS ARE ALL ABOUT PUSHING THE STORY FORWARD, ONE PANEL AT A
TIME. EACH PANEL ABOVE LEADS TO WHATEVER LIES BEHIND EACH DOOR.

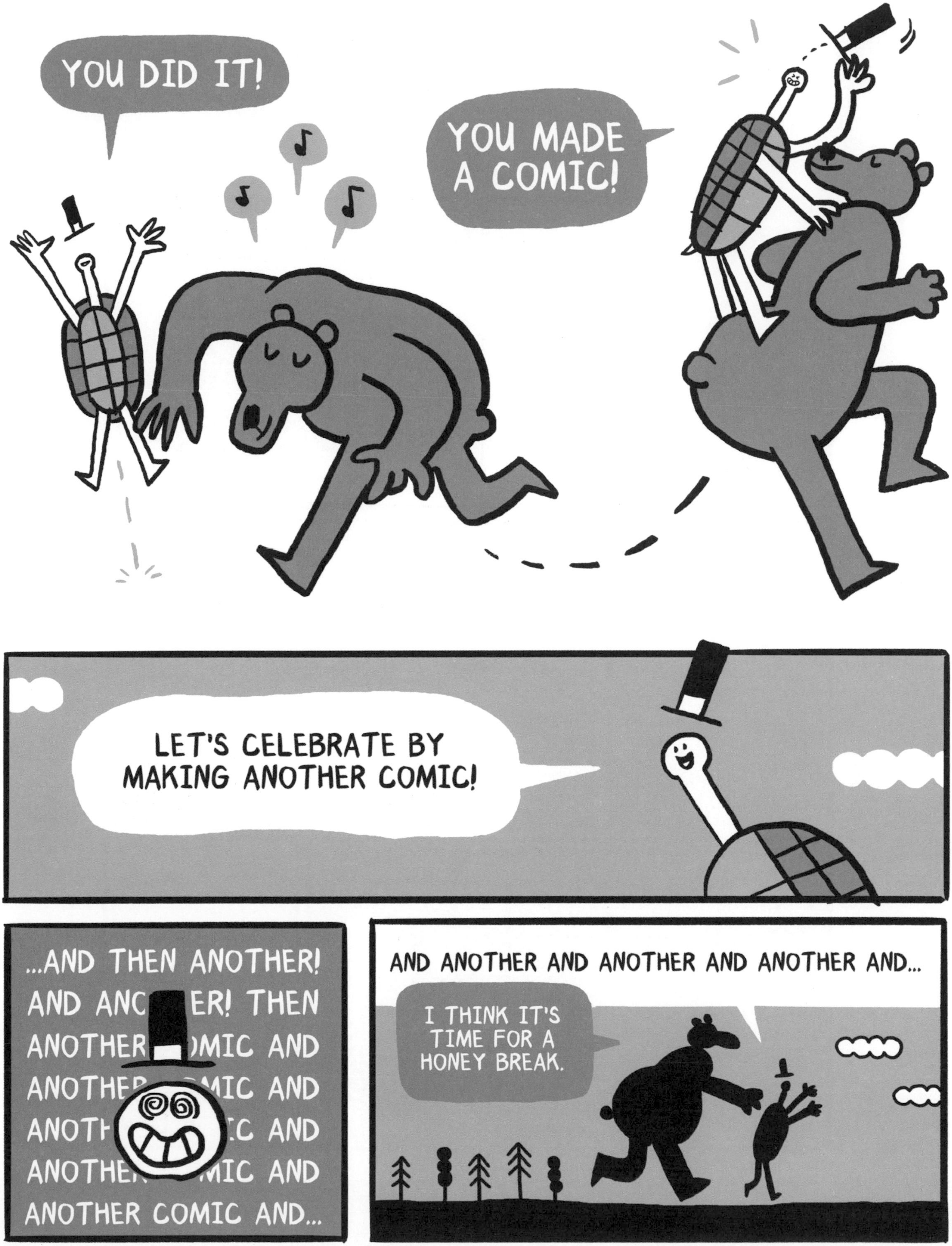
YOU DID IT!
YOU MADE A COMIC!
LET'S CELEBRATE BY MAKING ANOTHER COMIC!
...AND THEN ANOTHER! AND ANOTHER! THEN ANOTHER COMIC AND ANOTHER COMIC AND ANOTHER COMIC AND ANOTHER COMIC AND ANOTHER COMIC AND...
AND ANOTHER AND ANOTHER AND ANOTHER AND...
I THINK IT'S TIME FOR A HONEY BREAK.

WHAT DID YOU SAY?

I ALREADY TOLD YOU!

SPEECH BUBBLES SHOW US WHO IS TALKING AND WHAT THEY ARE SAYING. COMPLETE THE COMIC BELOW BY ADDING YOUR OWN WORDS TO PEANUT & BRAMBLE'S SPEECH BUBBLES.

BONUS: TRY IT WITH A FRIEND! ONE OF YOU CAN WRITE WHAT PEANUT SAYS AND THE OTHER CAN WRITE FOR BRAMBLE.

SOMETHING'S MISSING

LET'S FIND IT!

ADD EYEBROWS TO THE FACES BELOW TO SHOW
HOW PEANUT & BRAMBLE ARE FEELING.

JUST AS A SINGLE WORD CAN CHANGE THE MEANING OF A PANEL, THE POSITIONING
OF EYEBROWS CAN CHANGE THE MEANING OF A CHARACTER'S FACIAL EXPRESSION. ADD
EYEBROWS TO EACH CHARACTER AND WATCH THE MEANING CHANGE BEFORE YOUR EYES!

5

FRIENDLY TIME TRAVEL

SEND A FRIEND THROUGH TIME BY DRAWING THEM AS THEY MIGHT LOOK IN EACH OF THE TIME PERIODS LISTED BELOW.

FIVE YEARS AGO	NOW	IN FIVE YEARS	IN FIFTY YEARS

 HA HA--IT'S BABY BRAMBLE!

 LOOKING GOOD!

 BRAMBLE HAS A BEARD!

FIVE YEARS AGO	NOW	IN FIVE YEARS	IN FIFTY YEARS

DRAW MY CHARACTER

NO... DRAW MINE!

MY CHARACTER IS A TWELVE-YEAR-OLD GIRL WHO LIKES MUSIC AND LOVES TO CHANGE HER CLOTHES THREE TIMES A DAY. SHE HAS A PET HEDGEHOG AND LOTS OF FRECKLES.

WELL, MY CHARACTER IS A BUFF GUY WHO LIVES IN THE JUNGLE AND EATS BUGS. HE'S FROM THE FUTURE, WEARS A SHINY SUIT, AND HANGS OUT WITH ROBOTS.

A GREAT COMIC NEEDS GREAT CHARACTERS, AND A GREAT ARTIST
SHOULD BE ABLE TO TAKE DIRECTION FROM THE WRITER'S DESCRIPTIONS.

LIST MAKER

MAKE LISTS OF YOUR FAVORITE THINGS FOR EACH CATEGORY
BELOW. TRY TO FILL THE ENTIRE PAGE WITH YOUR FAVORITES!

PEOPLE

FOOD

GAMES

COMICS/
BOOKS

MOVIES

ACTIVITIES

 GENERATING IDEAS FOR CHARACTERS AND STORIES CAN BE AS EASY AS MAKING
LISTS OF THINGS YOU LIKE. YOU'LL AUTOMATICALLY WANT TO PICK THE BEST
ITEMS FROM YOUR LISTS, AND YOU CAN THEN COMBINE THEM TO MAKE SUPER-IDEAS!

WHAT'S HAPPENING?

NOT MUCH
TO SEE HERE...

NOW IS YOUR CHANCE TO CREATE YOUR OWN CHARACTER AND STORY BY COMPLETING THIS
SIX-PANEL COMIC! TAKE ONE OF THE CHARACTERS ON PAGE 7 AND PUT THEM IN A STORY
WITH SOME OF YOUR FAVORITE ITEMS FROM THE LIST-MAKER ACTIVITY ON PAGE 8.

MAKING A COMIC CAN BE AS SIMPLE AS STARTING WITH ONE PAGE
AND SIX PANELS. IS YOURS A COMPLETE STORY, OR COULD IT BE
THE BEGINNING OF YOUR FIRST GRAPHIC NOVEL OR COMIC BOOK?

9

HOW ARE YOU FEELING?

I FEEL FUZZY.

CAN YOU TELL HOW PEANUT & BRAMBLE ARE FEELING? WRITE ONE WORD
THAT DESCRIBES HOW THEY ARE FEELING IN EACH PICTURE BELOW.

PEANUT FEELS

_____

BRAMBLE FEELS

_____

PEANUT FEELS

_____

BRAMBLE FEELS

_____

PEANUT FEELS

_____

BRAMBLE FEELS

_____

FACIAL EXPRESSIONS CAN TELL THE READER A LOT ABOUT THE
WAY A CHARACTER IS FEELING. A LITTLE SMILE OR FROWN
CAN GO A LONG WAY IN MAKING A GREAT COMIC!

INK THIS PANEL

LET'S INK!

I'VE ALREADY DRAWN THIS PANEL IN BLUE PENCIL LINES. USE A PEN, MARKER, OR BRUSH TO DRAW OVER THE BLUE LINES IN INK. (THIS IS CALLED <u>INKING</u> YOUR COMIC!)

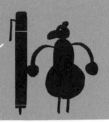

INKING IS WHERE AN ARTIST DRAWS OVER A PENCIL DRAWING IN INK TO MAKE THE "FINAL" LINE ART THAT READERS WILL SEE IN THE FINISHED COMIC. PAY ATTENTION TO THE TEXTURES THAT EACH BRUSH, PEN, AND MARKER MAKES. WHICH INKING TOOL DO YOU LIKE THE BEST? WHY?

11

INSIDE THE BORDER

THIS IS BORDERLINE AWESOME!

DRAW PANELS AROUND EACH PART OF THE COMIC BELOW.
PANELS ARE OFTEN RECTANGULAR, BUT YOU CAN MAKE THEM ANY SHAPE OR SIZE.

DRAW BORDERS AROUND THESE PANELS.

PANELS ARE TYPICALLY THOSE SQUARES YOU SEE IN A LOT OF COMICS, BUT THEY DON'T HAVE TO BE SQUARES.

RIGHT, BRAMBLE?

?

PANELS CAN BE ROUND OR SQUARE, ROUGH OR SMOOTH...

!

BIG OR SMALL...

...THICK OR THIN.

LOOSELY DRAWN OR MEASURED AND EXACT.

PANELS HELP BREAK UP A STORY INTO BITS SO IT DOESN'T ALL APPEAR TO HAPPEN AT ONCE--

MMM

YOM

...BRAM?

MMM

GLP!

SHLRMP

DID YOU HEAR ANYTHING I JUST SAID?!

MMM

HONEY

End!

PANELS HELP TO BREAK UP A STORY INTO SECTIONS AND SMALLER MOMENTS SO THE READER CAN EASILY UNDERSTAND WHAT IS HAPPENING AND WHEN IT IS HAPPENING. PANEL SHAPES AND SIZES CAN CHANGE THE MEANING OF A COMIC.

12

...AND THEN WHAT?

HMM...

COMPLETE THIS COMIC BY FILLING IN THE EMPTY PANELS WITH YOUR OWN WORDS AND DRAWINGS.

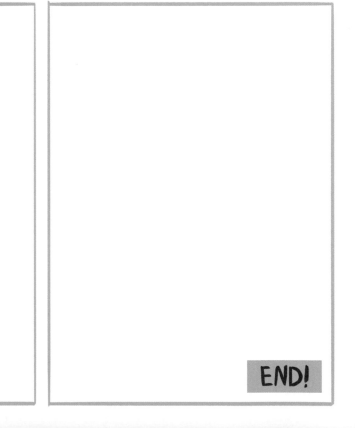

END!

LET'S MAKE FACES

BLEH!

TURN THE SHAPES BELOW INTO FACES BY ADDING EYES, EARS, AND OTHER FACIAL FEATURES. TURN THE SHAPES INTO YOUR CHOICE OF ANIMAL FACES, HUMAN FACES, ROBOT FACES, OR ALIEN FACES.

BONUS: GRAB SOME PAPER AND DRAW YOUR OWN SHAPES.
TAKE TURNS FILLING IN FACES ON THOSE NEW SHAPES WITH YOUR FRIENDS!

14

ONCE, BUT, AND

MAKE A SIMPLE THREE-PANEL COMIC TELLING AN ENTIRE STORY. INTRODUCE YOUR CHARACTER AND STORY IN PANEL 1 (ONCE), THEN MAKE A TWIST OR PROBLEM IN PANEL 2 (BUT). FINALLY, CREATE AN ENDING FOR YOUR COMIC IN PANEL 3 (AND).

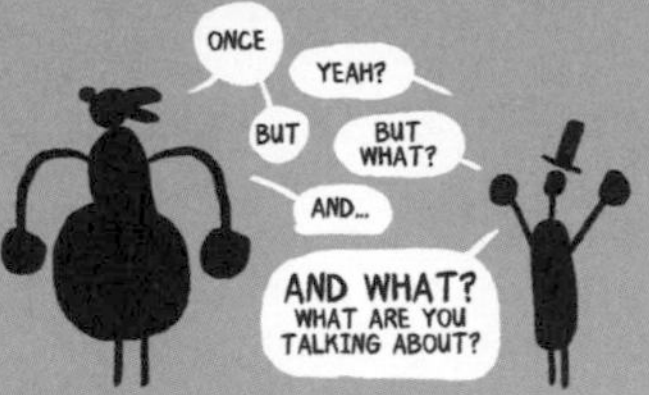

ONCE
YEAH?
BUT
BUT WHAT?
AND...
AND WHAT?
WHAT ARE YOU TALKING ABOUT?

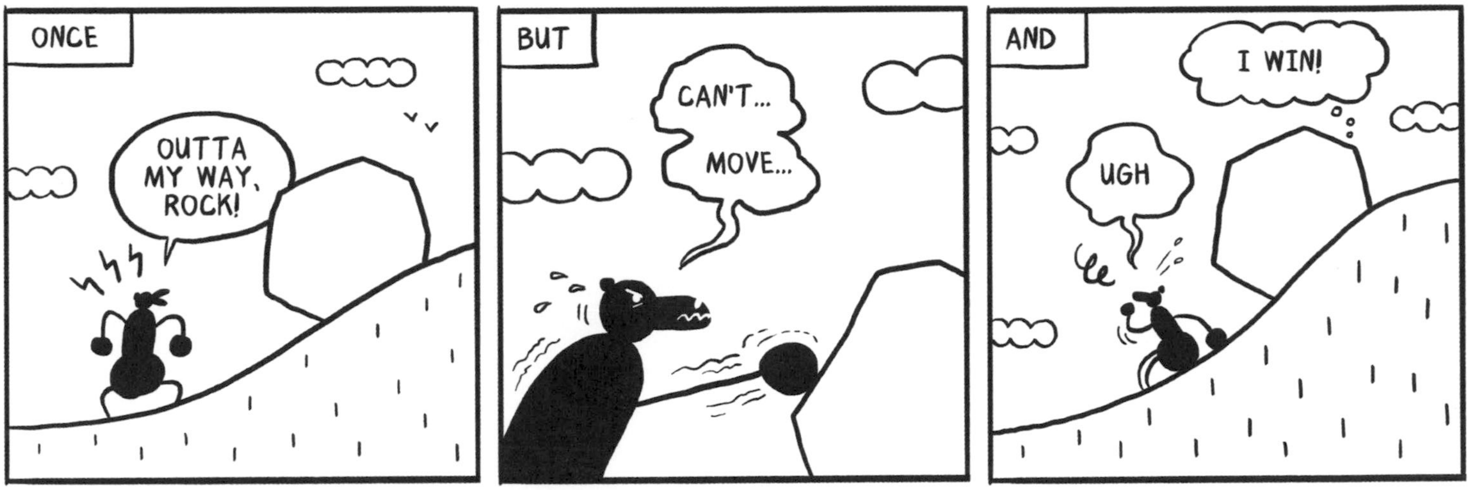

ONCE
OUTTA MY WAY, ROCK!
BUT
CAN'T...
MOVE...
AND
I WIN!
UGH

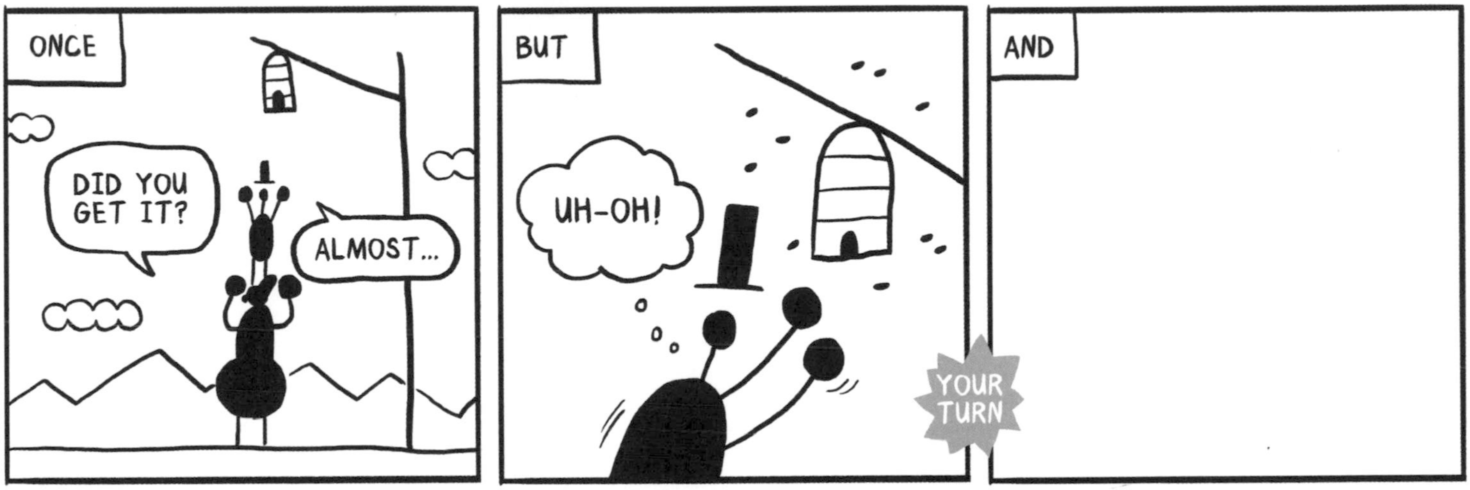

ONCE
DID YOU GET IT?
ALMOST...
BUT
UH-OH!
AND
YOUR TURN

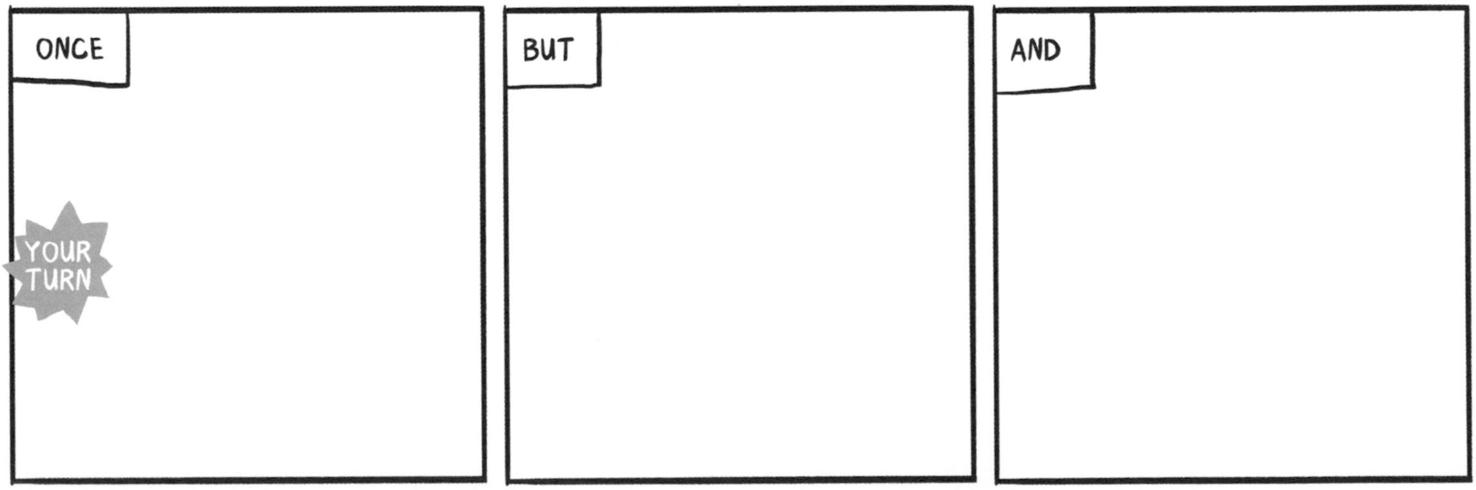

ONCE
BUT
AND
YOUR TURN

BONUS: DO ANY OF YOUR THREE-PANEL COMICS WORK IF YOU READ THEM BACKWARD? TRY DRAWING WHAT HAPPENS AFTER THE THIRD PANEL (EITHER GOING FORWARD OR BACKWARD IN THE STORY).

STEP-BY-STEP COMICS

HELP PEANUT & BRAMBLE MAKE THE FOLLOWING "HOW TO" COMICS BY WRITING
SIMPLE DIRECTIONS AND DRAWING SIMPLE PICTURES TO ACCOMPANY EACH ACTIVITY.

HOW TO
MAKE A
PEANUT BUTTER
AND JELLY
SANDWICH

BY PEANUT

① First, get two pieces of bread*

*whole wheat is my favorite!

② Put peanut butter on one piece and jelly on the other.

CAREFUL
P.B utter
Jelly
crunchy   Plum

③ Put both pieces together, and... EAT IT!!!

Yum!   very eat-able!

HOW TO
BRUSH
YOUR TEETH

BY

_____
(YOUR NAME HERE)

YOUR TURN!

1

2

3

MAKE YOUR OWN "HOW TO" COMIC BELOW, STARTING WITH THE TITLE. YOUR COMIC CAN BE ABOUT
ANYTHING: PLAYING SPORTS, DRAWING, DOING MATH, PLAYING MUSIC, MAKING THE BED, RIDING A BICYCLE,
MAKING A DRINK, FLYING AN AIRPLANE, DANCING, TALKING TO ALIENS, OR WALKING THE DOG.

COMICS AREN'T JUST FOR TELLING STORIES--THEY CAN ALSO BE INFORMATIONAL.
BECAUSE COMICS USE WORDS AND PICTURES TOGETHER, THEY CAN SHOW SOME
INFORMATION AND DESCRIBE OR EXPLAIN OTHER INFORMATION.

LET'S FACE IT ? FACE WHAT?

PEANUT & BRAMBLE ARE MISSING SOMETHING. CAN YOU ADD
APPROPRIATE FACIAL EXPRESSIONS TO EACH FACE BELOW?

HAPPY

SLEEPY

CONFUSED

ANGRY

GOOFY

SCARED

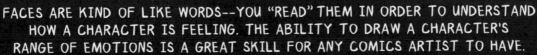

 FACES ARE KIND OF LIKE WORDS--YOU "READ" THEM IN ORDER TO UNDERSTAND
HOW A CHARACTER IS FEELING. THE ABILITY TO DRAW A CHARACTER'S
RANGE OF EMOTIONS IS A GREAT SKILL FOR ANY COMICS ARTIST TO HAVE.

17

PRETEND YOU ARE FILMING THIS COMIC WITH A CAMERA. MOVING THE CAMERA CLOSER AND FURTHER AWAY HELPS TO TELL YOUR STORY BY SHOWING WHAT IS MOST IMPORTANT IN EACH "SHOT" OR PANEL. WHICH PANELS FROM ROWS 1, 2, AND 3 BELOW TELL THE BEST STORY?

① PICK AND INK YOUR FAVORITE PANEL FROM EACH ROW BELOW. ② CUT OUT EACH INKED PANEL.
③ GLUE THE INKED PANELS INTO THE DOTTED PANEL SPACES BELOW TO COMPLETE YOUR COMIC!

INK AND CUT OUT YOUR FAVORITE PANELS, THEN GLUE THEM HERE. →

PANEL 1 GOES HERE

PANEL 2 GOES HERE

PANEL 3 GOES HERE

CLOSE-UP

WHEN THE "CAMERA" (OR VIEWER'S EYE) IS VERY CLOSE TO WHATEVER IT IS RECORDING. YOU ONLY SEE WHAT THE "CAMERA" SEES.

MEDIUM SHOT

WHEN THE "CAMERA" IS PULLED BACK A LITTLE FURTHER THAN WITH A CLOSE-UP SHOT.

WIDE SHOT

WHEN THE "CAMERA" IS FAR ENOUGH AWAY TO SHOW YOUR ENTIRE CHARACTER AND THEIR ENVIRONMENT.

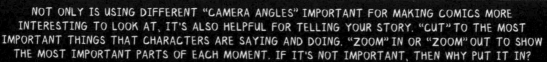
NOT ONLY IS USING DIFFERENT "CAMERA ANGLES" IMPORTANT FOR MAKING COMICS MORE INTERESTING TO LOOK AT, IT'S ALSO HELPFUL FOR TELLING YOUR STORY. "CUT" TO THE MOST IMPORTANT THINGS THAT CHARACTERS ARE SAYING AND DOING. "ZOOM" IN OR "ZOOM" OUT TO SHOW THE MOST IMPORTANT PARTS OF EACH MOMENT. IF IT'S NOT IMPORTANT, THEN WHY PUT IT IN?

LETTERING **AND INKING**

USING A PEN, MARKER, OR BRUSH, INK THE QUOTE BELOW, AND THEN
DECORATE THE SURROUNDING PAGE WITH DRAWINGS AND PATTERNS.

" WITH
WORDS
& PICTURES,
YOU CAN DO
JUST ABOUT
ANYTHING. "

-BILL WATTERSON
(CREATOR OF CALVIN AND HOBBES)

IT'S IMPORTANT TO WRITE USING NEAT AND CLEAN LETTERS SO THAT
OTHERS CAN READ YOUR GREAT COMIC. USING A PEN, BRUSH, OR MARKER
CAN HELP MAKE YOUR LETTERS EASY TO READ AND UNDERSTAND.

SAY WHAT?!

I..... ...I'M SPEECHLESS.

FIND A WARM PLACE AND COMPLETE THE COMIC BY ADDING
YOUR OWN WORDS TO PEANUT & BRAMBLE'S SPEECH BUBBLES.

END!

COMICS ARE WHAT HAPPENS WHEN PICTURES AND WORDS WORK
TOGETHER TO TELL A STORY. ADD DIFFERENT DIALOGUE TO EACH
BLANK SPEECH BUBBLE AND ENJOY THE WAY IT CHANGES THE STORY!

CAPTIONS TELL THE READER SOMETHING ABOUT WHAT IS HAPPENING IN THE PANEL.
ADD CAPTIONS TO COMPLETE EACH OF THE CARTOONS BELOW.

...THAT'S WHEN PEANUT REALIZED HIS SHELL WAS ON INSIDE OUT.

COMICS ARE A GREAT WAY TO MAKE "GAGS," OR SHORT, FUNNY, ONE-PANEL COMICS.
IT'S A SKILL TO TELL AN ENTIRE JOKE USING ONLY ONE PANEL AND A HANDFUL OF WORDS.

LINE PLAYGROUND

WHOA!

COMPLETE EACH OF THE DRAWING CHALLENGES BELOW. TRY DRAWING WITH
A PEN <u>AND</u> A BRUSH FOR EACH CHALLENGE--IT'S TRICKIER THAN IT SEEMS!

DRAW THIS HOUSE, USING ONLY
ONE LINE. DON'T LIFT YOUR PEN,
AND DON'T RETRACE ANY
LINES YOU'VE ALREADY MADE.

PICK A LETTER TO DRAW,
THEN OUTLINE THE SHAPE OF
YOUR LETTER OVER AND OVER.

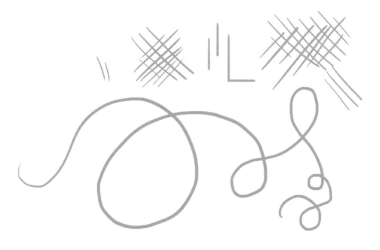

MAKE A DOT AND SPIRAL.
KEEP YOUR LINES CLOSE,
BUT DON'T LET THEM TOUCH!

MAKE SOME SQUIGGLY LINES, CURVY LINES,
STRAIGHT LINES, CRISS-CROSS LINES, AND SO ON.

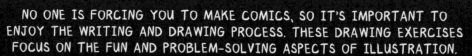

MORE DRAMA!!!

YEESH. — SO DRAMATIC.

REDRAW EACH OF THE PANELS AND CHARACTERS IN THE COMICS BELOW TO MAKE THEM MORE DRAMATIC. FEEL FREE TO CHANGE "CAMERA ANGLES" AND DIALOGUE.

DOT, DO YOU LIKE COMICS?

YES.

WE LIKE COMICS, TOO.

SUPER-SMART BEAR IS MY FAVORITE.

MAKE YOUR PANELS MORE EXCITING AND DRAMATIC BY USING FACIAL EXPRESSIONS AND BODY LANGUAGE. YOU CAN ALSO USE CLOSE-UPS, MEDIUM SHOTS, AND WIDE SHOTS TO SHOW THE MOST IMPORTANT AND EXCITING PARTS OF YOUR COMIC.

YOUR COMIC GOES DOWN HERE!

OOH--DRAMATIC!

NOW **THAT'S** DRAMA!

 BONUS: USING A SEPARATE SHEET OF PAPER, MAKE A COMIC THAT TELLS WHAT HAPPENS NEXT.

23

SET THE LINES FREE LET THEM GO!

THIS WHOLE PAGE IS FOR YOU TO TRY OUT YOUR BRUSHES AND PENS!
DRAW AND WRITE WHATEVER YOU'D LIKE--BUT MAKE SURE YOU FILL THE WHOLE PAGE!

LOOPY

THIN

LONG

THICK

ROUGH

STRAIGHT

SMOOTH

WIGGLY

SHORT

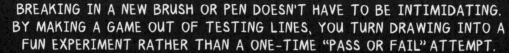
BREAKING IN A NEW BRUSH OR PEN DOESN'T HAVE TO BE INTIMIDATING.
BY MAKING A GAME OUT OF TESTING LINES, YOU TURN DRAWING INTO A
FUN EXPERIMENT RATHER THAN A ONE-TIME "PASS OR FAIL" ATTEMPT.

24

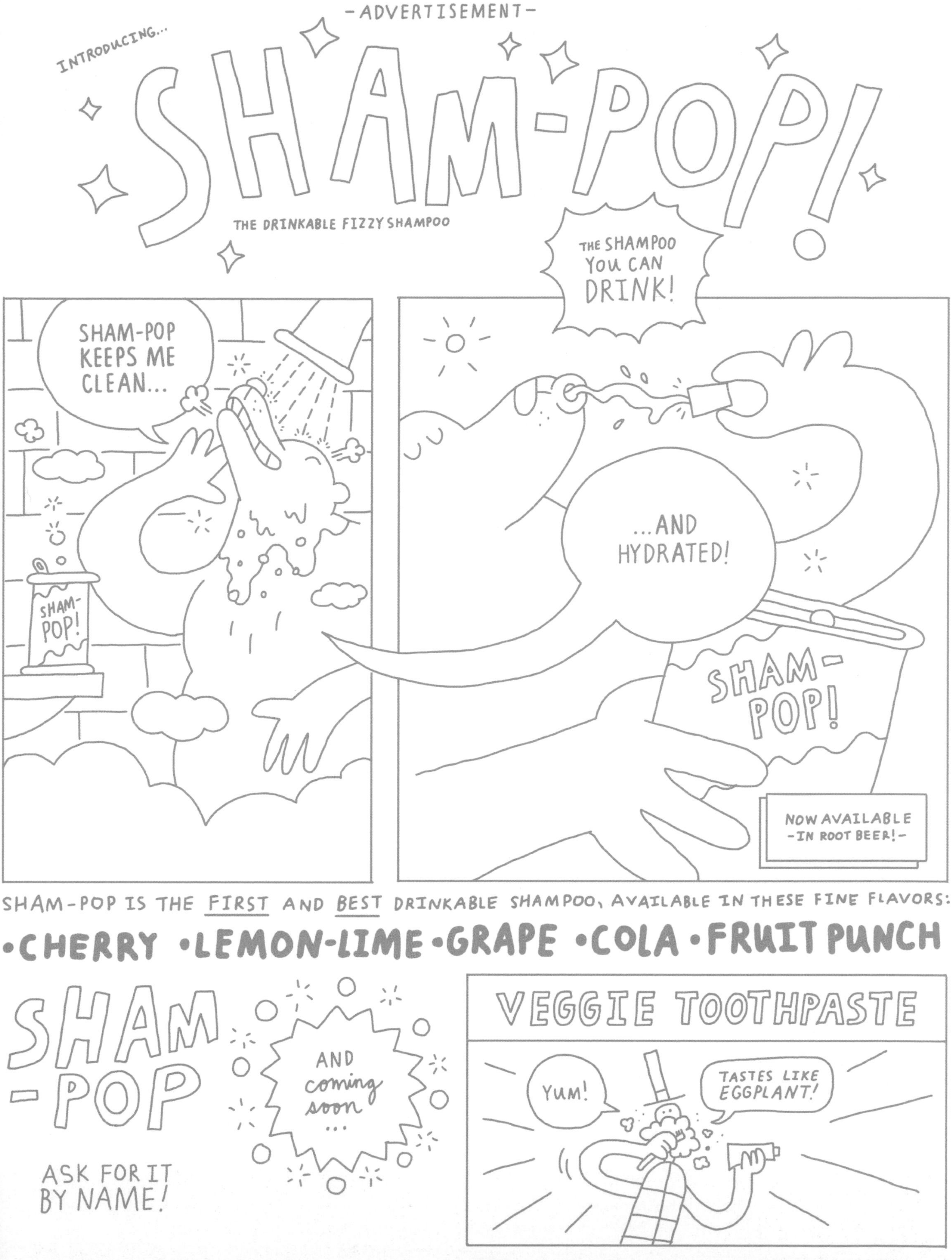
-ADVERTISEMENT-
INTRODUCING...
SHAM-POP!
THE DRINKABLE FIZZY SHAMPOO
THE SHAMPOO YOU CAN DRINK!
SHAM-POP KEEPS ME CLEAN...
SHAM-POP!
...AND HYDRATED!
SHAM-POP!
NOW AVAILABLE -IN ROOT BEER!-
SHAM-POP IS THE FIRST AND BEST DRINKABLE SHAMPOO, AVAILABLE IN THESE FINE FLAVORS:
•CHERRY •LEMON-LIME •GRAPE •COLA •FRUIT PUNCH
SHAM-POP
AND coming soon...
ASK FOR IT BY NAME!
VEGGIE TOOTHPASTE
YUM!
TASTES LIKE EGGPLANT!

LET'S TAKE A WALK

UM...PEANUT?

WHERE ARE WE TAKING THIS WALK?

HELP PEANUT & BRAMBLE GO FOR A WALK IN THEIR FAVORITE FOREST BY DRAWING THE ENVIRONMENT AND BACKGROUND IN EACH PANEL. (IT MIGHT HELP TO DRAW IN PENCIL FIRST.)

BACKGROUNDS AND ENVIRONMENTS ARE A GREAT WAY TO SHOW WHERE YOUR COMIC TAKES PLACE WITHOUT USING ANY WORDS. A GOOD BACKGROUND STAYS IN THE BACKGROUND, WITHOUT DRAWING SPECIAL ATTENTION TO ITSELF.

AGAIN WITH THE DRAMA?!

OH, PUH-LEASE!

REDRAW EACH OF THE PANELS AND CHARACTERS IN THE COMICS BELOW TO MAKE THEM MORE DRAMATIC. FEEL FREE TO CHANGE "CAMERA ANGLES" AND DIALOGUE.

MAKE YOUR PANELS MORE EXCITING AND DRAMATIC BY ADDING BACKGROUNDS AND FACIAL EXPRESSIONS. TRY USING DIFFERENT "CAMERA ANGLES" AND CHANGING BODY LANGUAGE. YOU CAN EVEN CHANGE THE SHAPE AND SIZE OF SPEECH BUBBLES AND THE APPEARANCE OF WORDS. IT CAN ALSO HELP TO SHOW EACH CHARACTER DOING SOMETHING IN EACH PANEL--EVEN THE CHARACTERS THAT ARE PLACED IN THE BACKGROUND.

 FOCUSING ON THE MOST DRAMATIC PARTS OF YOUR COMIC WILL MAKE IT MORE EXCITING TO READ. IT'S ALSO MORE FUN TO WRITE AND DRAW THE MOST DRAMATIC PARTS OF A STORY.

CUTTING YOUR COMIC TO INCLUDE ONLY THE MOST IMPORTANT PARTS
KEEPS YOUR STORY MOVING FORWARD AND KEEPS THE READER INTERESTED.

STUFFED COMICS

MMM...
STUFFING.

IT'S THE STUFFING THAT MAKES THESE COMICS SO TASTY! ADD WORDS AND
PICTURES TO THE MISSING MIDDLE PANELS BELOW TO COMPLETE EACH COMIC.

WHILE IT CAN BE BORING FOR A READER TO SEE EVERYTHING THAT HAPPENS TO
A CHARACTER, IT'S IMPORTANT TO SHOW ENOUGH FOR THE READER TO UNDERSTAND
WHAT HAPPENS AND HOW IT LEADS TO THE NEXT PART OF YOUR COMIC.

STOP EVERYTHING

READ THE COMIC BELOW. PAY CLOSE ATTENTION TO THE "SILENT" WORDLESS PANEL. THEN FOLLOW THE DIRECTIONS TO COMPLETE YOUR OWN COMIC!

 NOW YOU TRY! MAKE YOUR OWN FOUR-PANEL COMIC, AND LEAVE ONE PANEL WITHOUT ANY TALKING.

SOMETIMES THE MOST IMPORTANT PART OF A COMIC (TAKE A DEEP BREATH!) IS A MOMENT WITHOUT WORDS OR DRAMATIC ACTION. THE POWER OF A PAUSE COMES FROM WHERE AND HOW IT IS USED.

THE EMPTINESS

SO MUCH EMPTY...

FIGHT THE EMPTINESS BY FINISHING THIS COMIC! ADD YOUR OWN
DRAWINGS AND SPEECH BUBBLES TO COMPLETE THIS EIGHT-PANEL COMIC.

MAKING A COMIC CAN BE AS SIMPLE AS WRITING AND DRAWING ONE PANEL AT A TIME, OR
TELLING A STORY IN ONLY EIGHT PANELS. EVEN COMICS PROS START WITH A BLANK PAGE!

31

HOW TO DRAW PEENiT.

↓

BYE BRAMBL.

STEP ONE: DRAW A TERTLE.

STEP 2: PUT A HAT ON THE TERTLE.

I'M PEENiT!

I HOPE YOU LIKED MY COMIK AND NOW YOU CAN DRAW PEENiT.

ME →

IT'S RILL EAZY TO DRAW PEENiT. SO THAT'S WHY i MAID THIS COMIK.

EZ

SOMETIMEZ i MAIK COMIKS ABOUT MISELF.

(i'M SUPER SMART BEAR)

SMORT

↓

~~EAT HUN~~ SOMETIMEZ i'M SHY.

BUT i LIKE COMIKS, AND ~~SODE SOA~~ SODAZ PEENiT, TOO.

SUPER SMORT BEAR

↓

COMIK

SO, THAT'S MY COMIK. BIE!!

LET'S MAKE A... **SIXTEEN-PAGE ACCORDION-FOLD TEENSY-TINY MINI COMIC**

YOU WILL NEED: 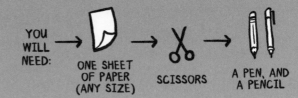 ONE SHEET OF PAPER (ANY SIZE) — SCISSORS — A PEN, AND A PENCIL

1 FOLD IN HALF FROM SIDE TO SIDE, AND THEN FOLD IN HALF AGAIN.

FOLD IN HALF FROM TOP TO BOTTOM, AND THEN IN HALF AGAIN.

2 UNFOLD AND NUMBER YOUR "PAGES" LIKE THIS.

(NOTICE THAT THESE ROWS ARE UPSIDE-DOWN.)

3 CUT CAREFULLY AND STOP LIKE SO.

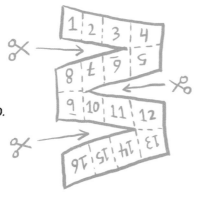

4 FOLD. 5 FOLDS UP INTO THE BACK OF 4.

BACK OF 12 FOLDS DOWN TO BACK OF 13.

BACK OF 8 FOLDS DOWN TO BACK OF 9.

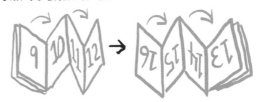

ADD COVERS AND WRITE/DRAW YOUR SIXTEEN-PAGE COMIC!

5

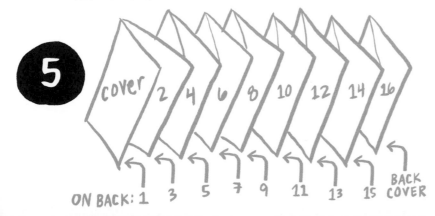

cover / 2 / 4 / 6 / 8 / 10 / 12 / 14 / 16

ON BACK: 1   3   5   7   9   11   13   15   BACK COVER

6 MAKE COPIES BY UNFOLDING YOUR PAPER.

× 100

SAVE ONE FOR ME!

COMICS COME IN ALL SHAPES AND SIZES. EACH FORMAT LENDS ITSELF TO A DIFFERENT KIND OF STORY AND READING EXPERIENCE FOR THE READER. PLUS, IT'S FUN TO TAKE A BREAK FROM WRITING AND DRAWING TO FOCUS ON FOLDING AND CUTTING PAPER!

1	2	3	4
8	7	6	5
9	10	11	12
16	15	14	13

1. DRAW A CIRCLE.

I LIKE CIRCLES!

2.

3. PUT A HILL ON TOP.

UM...WHAT ARE YOU DOING?

4.

5. ADD A CIRCLE WITH 2 LITTLE CIRCLES ON TOP.

ARE YOU SURE THIS IS RIGHT?

6.

7. ADD A SIDEWAYS HILL AND A CIRCLE FOR HIS TAIL.

I THINK HE'S MISSING SOMETHING.

8.

9. ADD SOME BRAMBLE-Y ARMS AND BALL HANDS.

I THINK I SEE IT...

10.

11. ...AND LEGS.

LOOKIN' GOOD!

12.

13. DON'T FORGET THAT FURRY BEAR FACE!

SO CLOSE...

14.

15. YOU JUST DREW A BRAMBLE!

HE LOOKS FAMILIAR!

16.

PEANUT & BRAMBLE

I'M
BIG

I'M
SMALL

(MAKE COPIES OF THIS COMIC
BY UNFOLDING IT ALL THE WAY.)

ADD THE SPEECH BUBBLES

COMPLETE THIS COMIC BY ADDING SPEECH BUBBLES, THOUGHT BUBBLES, AND CAPTIONS.
THINK ABOUT THE SHAPE AND SIZE OF EACH BUBBLE AND HOW IT HELPS TO TELL THE STORY.

THIS SIZE AND SHAPE OF A SPEECH BUBBLE CAN TELL THE READER MANY IMPORTANT THINGS: IF THE SPEAKER IS A ROBOT, IF THE SPEAKER IS EVIL OR FRIENDLY, OR IF THE SPEAKER IS WHISPERING. SPEECH BUBBLES CAN BE A GREAT WAY TO SHOW THE READER SOMETHING ABOUT THE CHARACTER THAT ISN'T OBVIOUS IN THE TEXT.

BEFORE AND AFTER

ONE PANEL IS MISSING FROM EACH COMIC BELOW.
ADD WORDS AND PICTURES SO THAT EACH COMIC MAKES SENSE!

IT'S IMPORTANT FOR READERS TO UNDERSTAND THE SEQUENCE OF
EVENTS IN YOUR COMIC. IF SOMETHING ISN'T CLEAR TO THE READER,
IT CAN BE CONFUSING AND WEAKEN THE STRENGTH OF YOUR COMIC.

READ MY LIPS

DRAW FACES AND EXPRESSIONS FOR EACH OF THE DRAWINGS IN THE COMICS BELOW. THINK ABOUT WHETHER THE FACES SHOULD BE HAPPY, SAD, GRUMPY, AND SO ON.

FACES ARE KIND OF LIKE BIG SIGNS THAT TELL READERS HOW YOUR CHARACTERS ARE FEELING. IF FACIAL EXPRESSIONS ARE ALWAYS THE SAME, YOU MISS A CHANCE TO SHOW READERS IMPORTANT INFORMATION ABOUT THE CHARACTERS' FEELINGS AND EMOTIONS.

SAME--BUT DIFFERENT

WHO'S DIFFERENT?

HOW MANY WAYS CAN YOU USE AND REUSE THE SAME IMAGE (OR PARTS OF IT) IN THE SAME FOUR-PANEL COMIC? FIND OUT BY ADDING WORDS AND COMPLETING THE COMICS BELOW!

WE'LL USE THIS DRAWING OF PEANUT FOR ALL FOUR PANELS OF THIS COMIC.

USE THIS DRAWING OF BRAMBLE TO COMPLETE THIS FOUR-PANEL COMIC

MAKE YOUR OWN! (BE SURE TO USE THE SAME DRAWING IN ALL FOUR PANELS)

WRITING AND DRAWING COMICS IS ALL ABOUT USING WORDS AND PICTURES TO TELL YOUR STORY. REUSING THE SAME DRAWING IN DIFFERENT WAYS HELPS TO DEMONSTRATE JUST HOW MUCH STORY A SINGLE PICTURE CONTAINS.

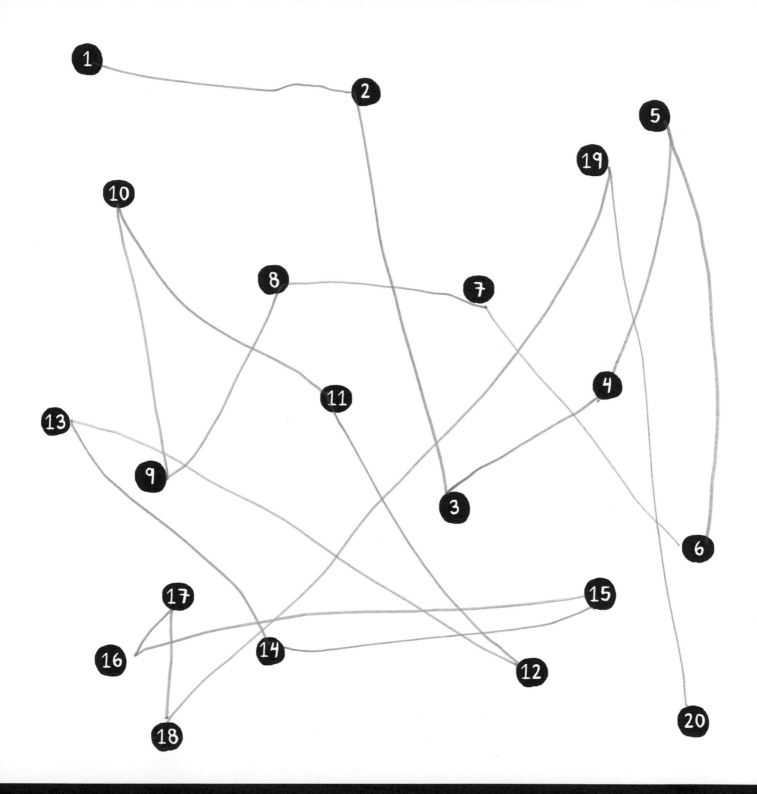

DOT TO DOT

DOT...

CONNECT THE DOTS IN ORDER, BUT WITHOUT USING STRAIGHT LINES! INSTEAD, CONNECT THE DOTS USING WIGGLY, LOOPING, AND ZIGZAGGING LINES.

UH!

CAVE DRAWING

UM...PEANUT? CAVES CAN'T DRAW.

MAKE YOUR OWN CAVE-DRAWING VERSIONS (OR STICK FIGURES) OF EACH OF THE DRAWINGS BELOW.

BRAMBLE

FLOWER

DOT

PEANUT

MAKING COMICS IS LESS ABOUT CREATING AMAZINGLY DETAILED DRAWINGS, AND MORE ABOUT MAKING DRAWINGS THAT ARE EASY FOR THE READER TO UNDERSTAND. A SIMPLE "CAVE DRAWING" APPROACH CAN BE USED TO CONVEY POWERFUL STORIES IN WAYS THAT DETAILED DRAWINGS CAN'T!

CAVE COMIC

ME LIKE CAVE COMIC!

COMPLETE THE COMIC BELOW BY ADDING SIMPLE "CAVE DRAWINGS" OR STICK FIGURE IMAGES.

HEY, PEANUT...DO YOU THINK DOT WILL LIKE THESE FLOWERS?

OF COURSE SHE WILL, BRAMBLE!

...ESPECIALLY **THIS** ONE!

OOH--HONEY!

HEY, PEANUT.

OH-- HI, DOT!

GASP!

IS THAT FLOWER FOR ME?

UM...

THAT'S SO SWEET!

I LOVE IT!

SOME SCHOLARS POINT TO CAVE DRAWINGS AS THE FIRST COMICS. SIMPLE SHAPES AND LINES CAN TELL POWERFUL STORIES, EVEN WHEN VIEWED THOUSANDS OF YEARS AFTER THEIR CREATION!

43

MISSING PANELS

I MISS THEM SO MUCH!

SOME OF THE PANELS ARE MISSING FROM THE COMIC BELOW!
WRITE AND DRAW IN EACH EMPTY PANEL TO COMPLETE THE COMIC.

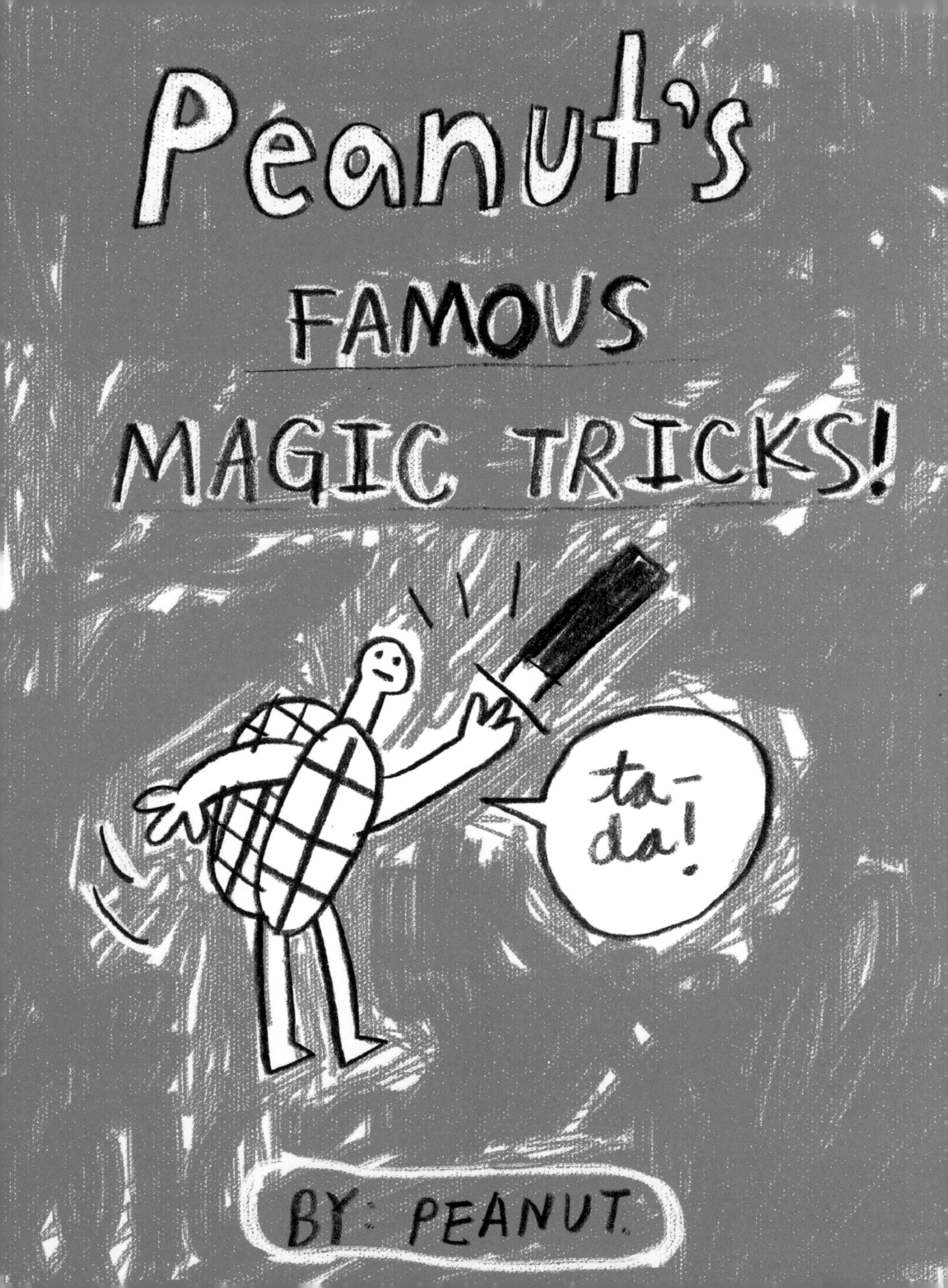
Peanut's
FAMOUS
MAGIC TRICKS!
ta-da!
BY: PEANUT.

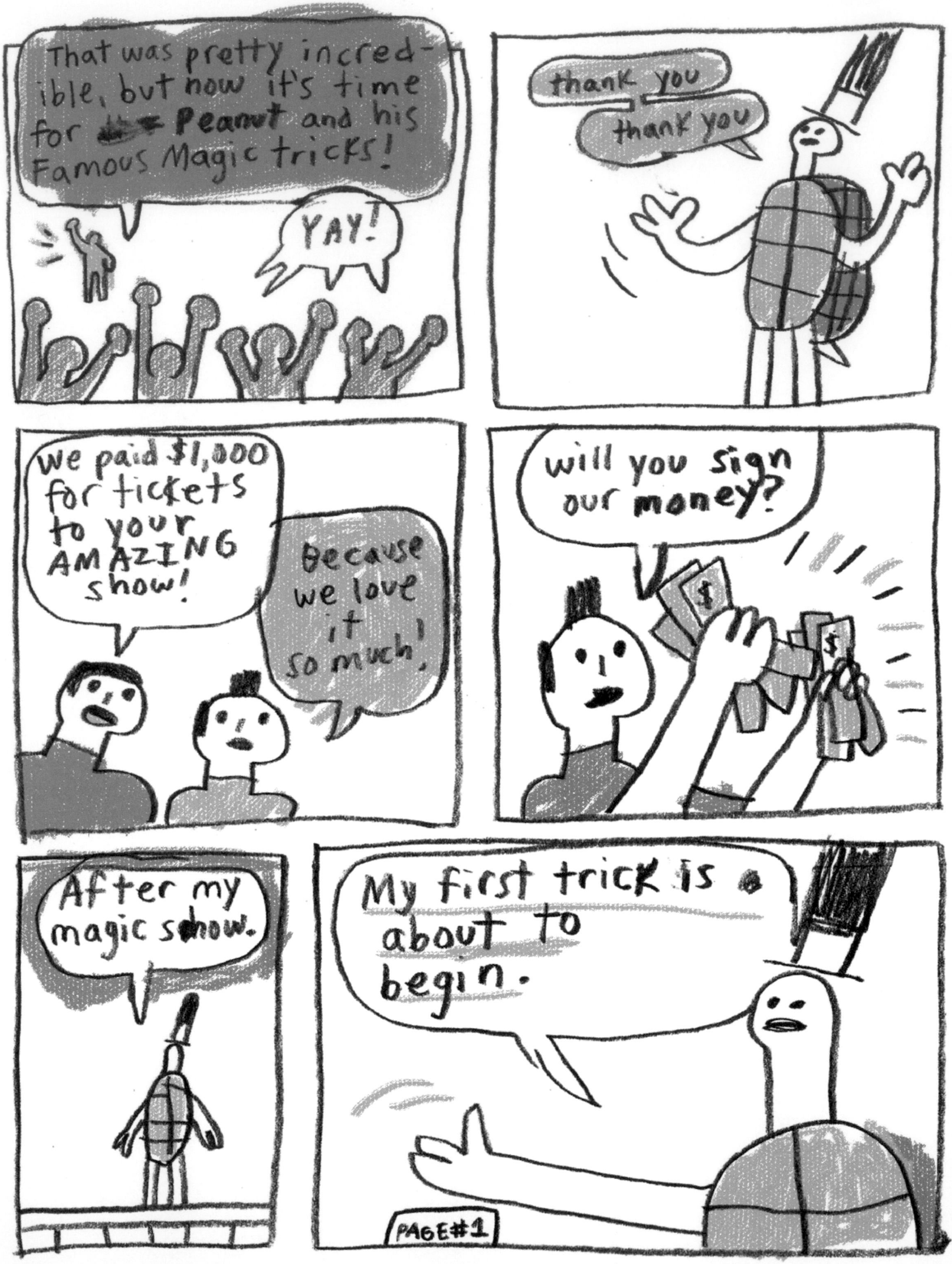
That was pretty incredible, but now it's time for Peanut and his Famous Magic tricks!
YAY!
thank you
thank you
We paid $1,000 for tickets to your AMAZING show!
Because we love it so much!
will you sign our money?
After my magic show.
My first trick is about to begin.
PAGE#1

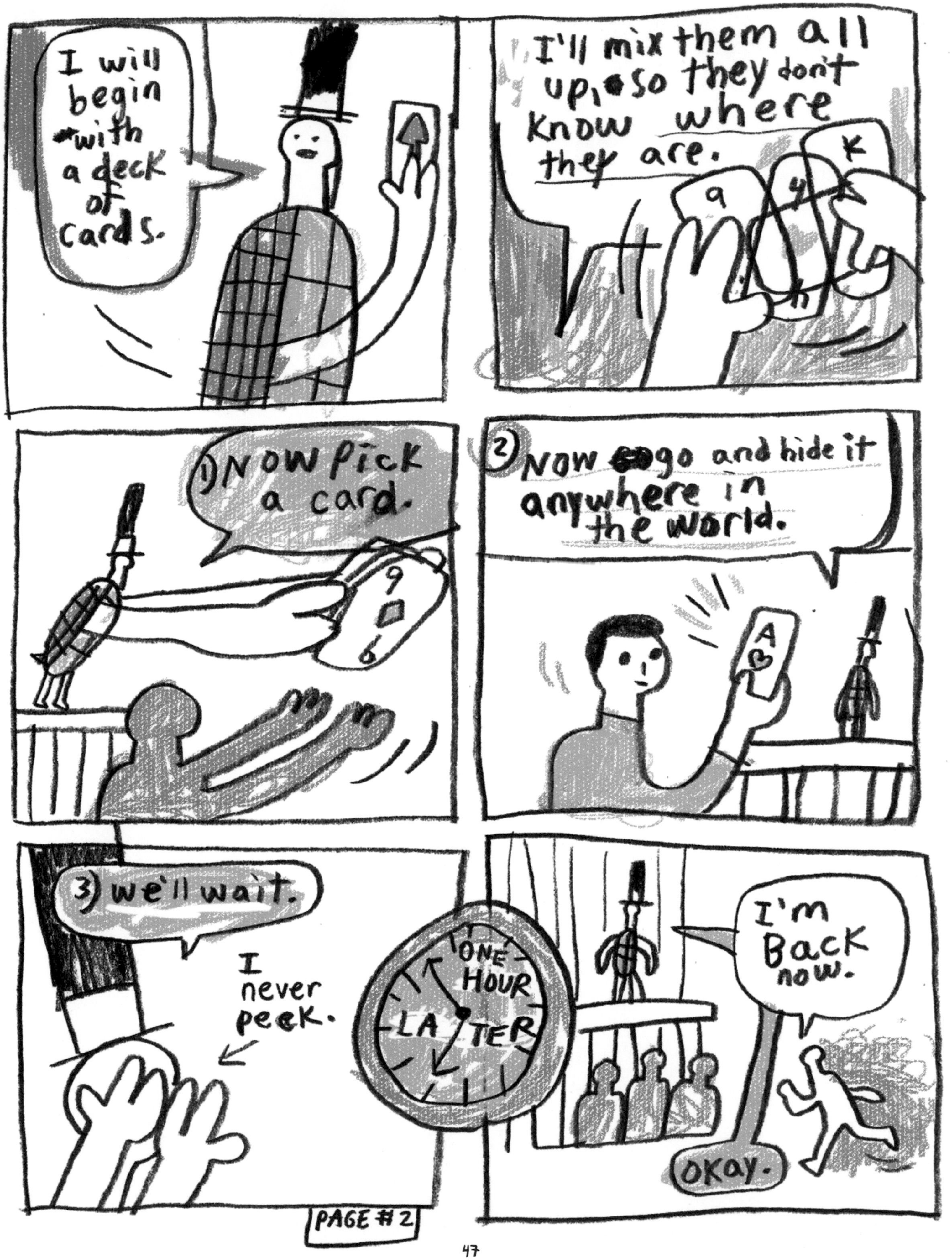
I will begin with a deck of cards.
I'll mix them all up, so they don't know where they are.
1) Now pick a card.
2) Now go and hide it anywhere in the world.
3) we'll wait.
I never peek.
ONE HOUR LATER
I'm Back now.
Okay.
PAGE #2

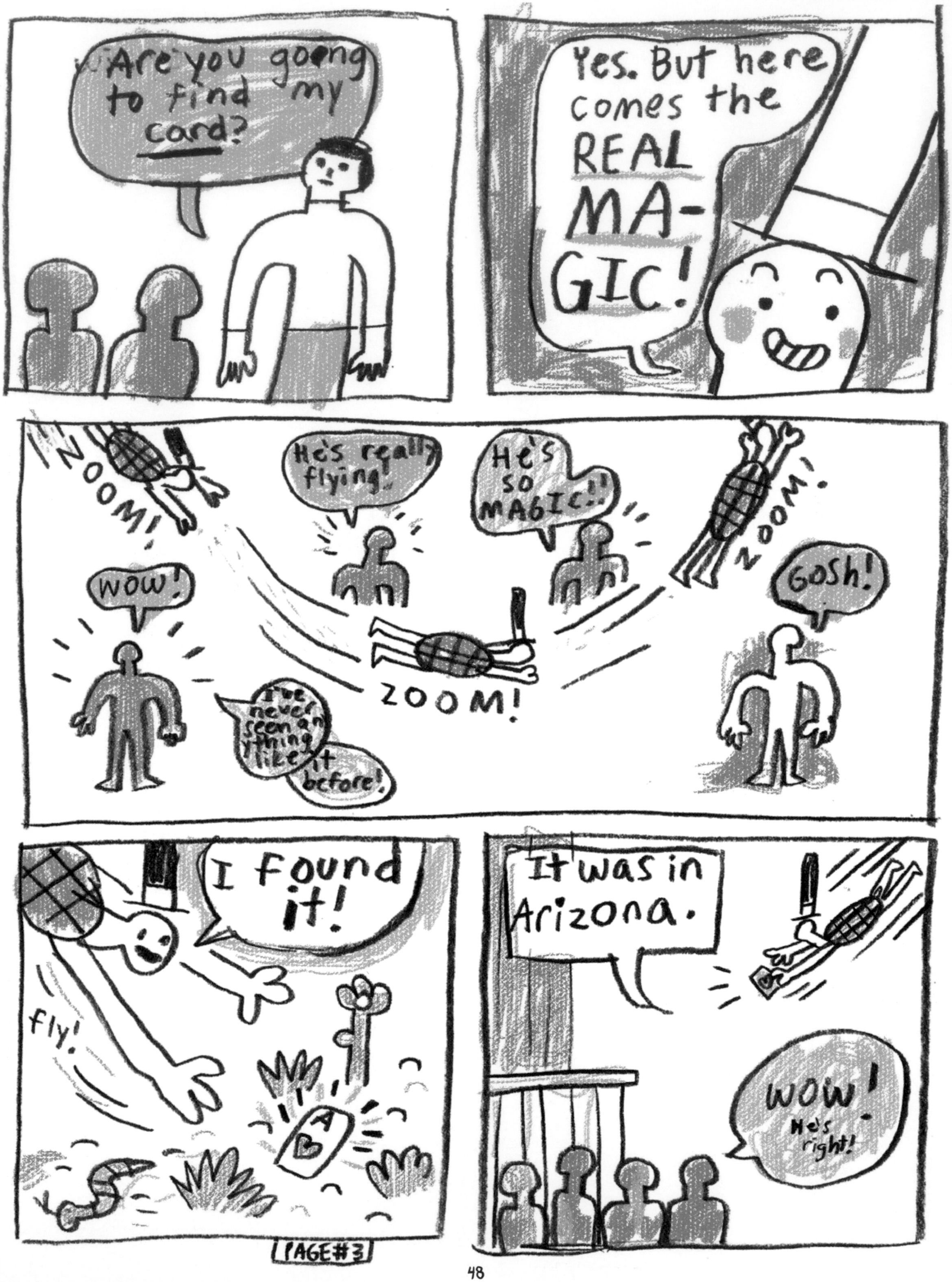

Are you going to find my card?
Yes. But here comes the REAL MA-GIC!
ZOOM!
He's really flying!
He's so MAGIC!!
ZOOM!
WOW!
GOSH!
ZOOM!
I've never seen anything like it before!
I found it!
fly!
A
It was in Arizona.
WOW! He's right!
PAGE#3

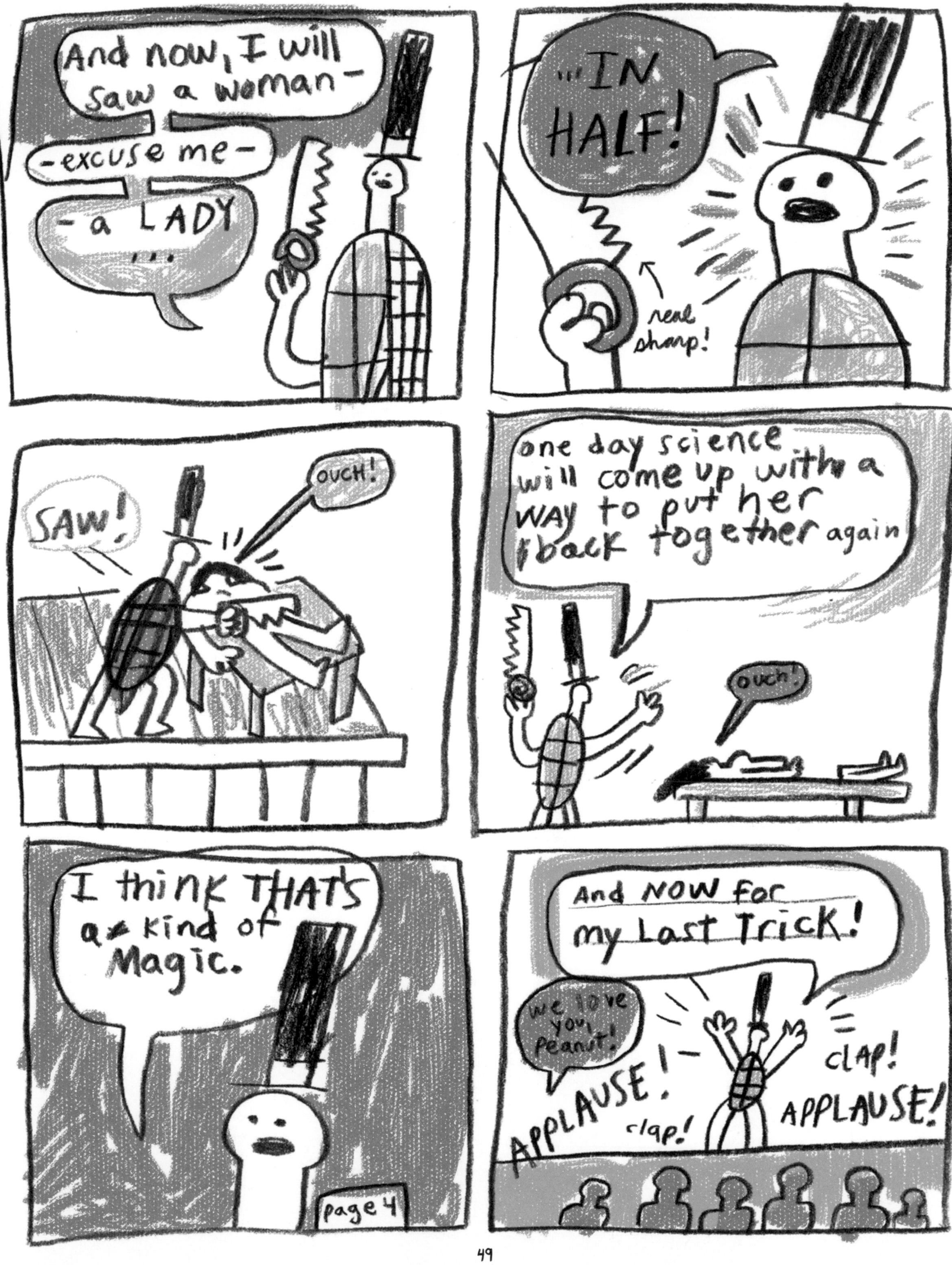

And now, I will saw a woman-
-excuse me-
-a LADY...
...IN HALF!
real sharp!
SAW!
OUCH!
one day science will come up with a way to put her back together again
ouch!
I think THAT'S a kind of Magic.
page 4
And NOW for my Last Trick!
We love you, Peanut!
APPLAUSE!
clap!
CLAP!
APPLAUSE!

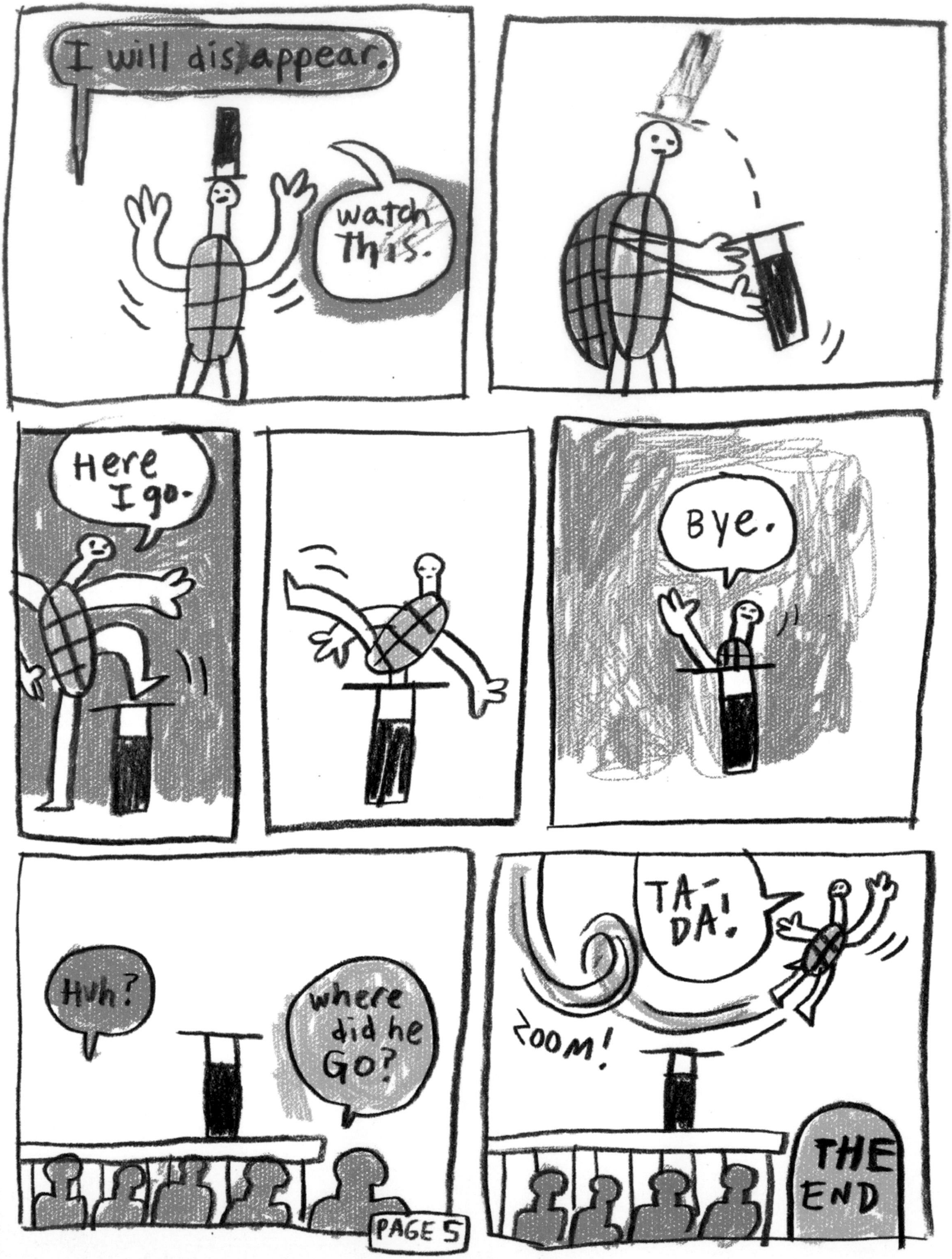
I will disappear.
watch this.
Here I go.
Bye.
Huh?
where did he Go?
PAGE 5
TA-DA!
ZOOM!
THE END

WHAT'S UNDER THERE?

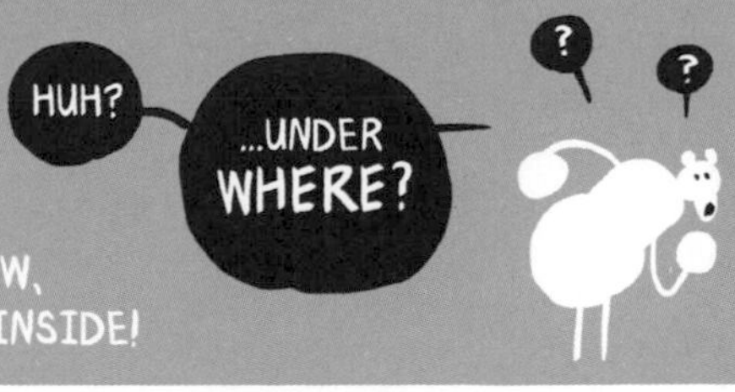
HUH?
...UNDER WHERE?

TAKE A LOOK AT WHAT'S INSIDE THE SANDWICHES BELOW,
THEN MAKE YOUR OWN SANDWICH BY DRAWING WHAT GOES INSIDE!

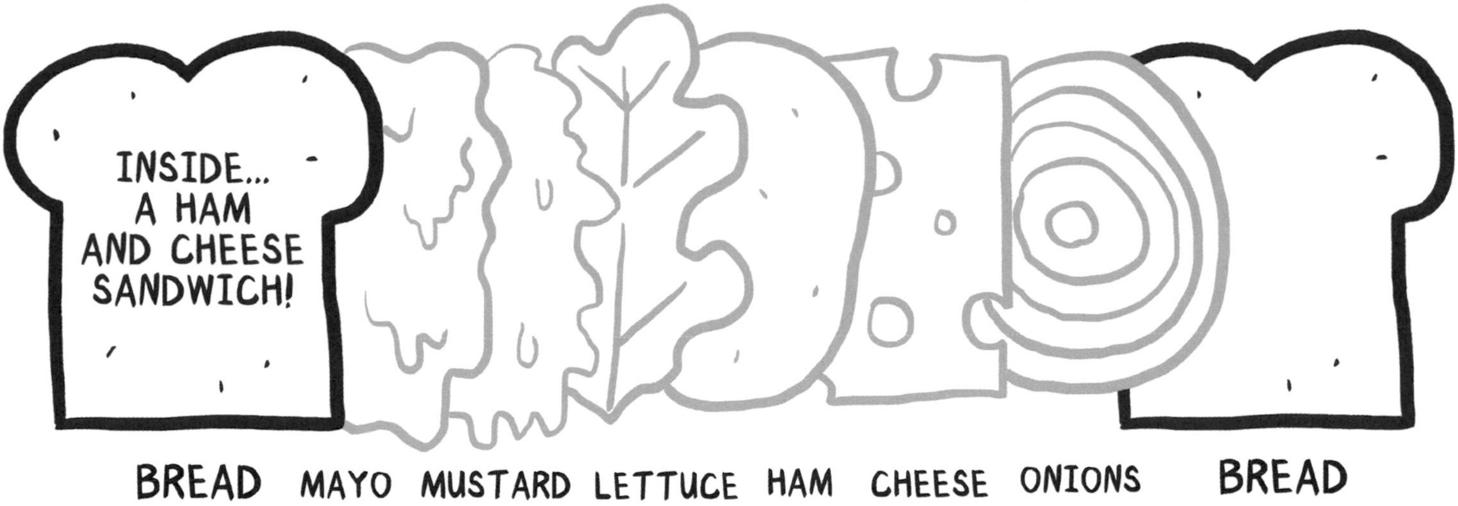
INSIDE... A HAM AND CHEESE SANDWICH!
BREAD
MAYO
MUSTARD
LETTUCE
HAM
CHEESE
ONIONS
BREAD

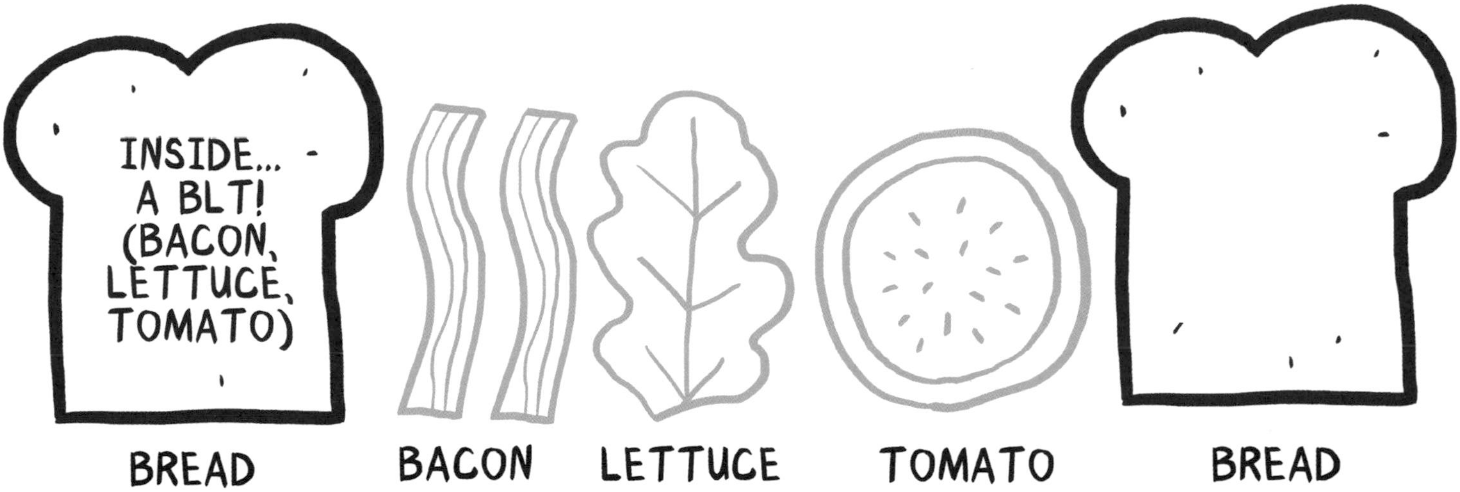
INSIDE... A BLT! (BACON, LETTUCE, TOMATO)
BREAD
BACON
LETTUCE
TOMATO
BREAD

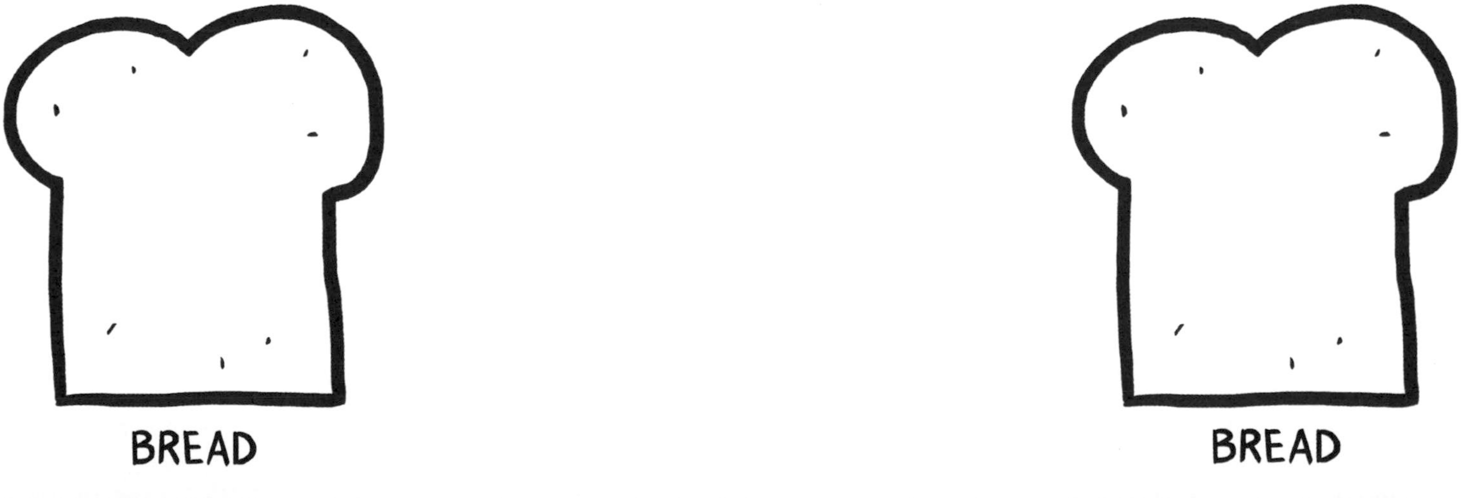
BREAD
BREAD

COMICS ARE GREAT FOR TELLING STORIES, GIVING DIRECTIONS, AND SHARING OTHER INFORMATION. IF YOU'VE EVER BEEN MESMERIZED BY A CHART, DIAGRAM, OR INFOGRAPHIC, THEN YOU ARE A WITNESS TO THE POWER OF WHAT CAN HAPPEN WHEN WORDS AND PICTURES WORK TOGETHER TO COMMUNICATE INFORMATION!

MAKE YOUR OWN ADVERTISEMENT

YOUR AD CAN BE FOR A FAKE PRODUCT OR SERVICE (SHAM-POP, ANYONE?), OR IT CAN BE FOR SOMETHING REAL, LIKE YOUR FAVORITE COMIC, SHOES, TACO, MOVIE, SPORTS TEAM, OR GAME!

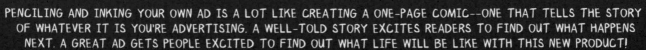

PENCILING AND INKING YOUR OWN AD IS A LOT LIKE CREATING A ONE-PAGE COMIC--ONE THAT TELLS THE STORY OF WHATEVER IT IS YOU'RE ADVERTISING. A WELL-TOLD STORY EXCITES READERS TO FIND OUT WHAT HAPPENS NEXT. A GREAT AD GETS PEOPLE EXCITED TO FIND OUT WHAT LIFE WILL BE LIKE WITH THIS NEW PRODUCT!

BOLD WORDS

I MEAN IT...

DID YOU STEP IN SOMETHING?

! I STINK!

PICK ONE WORD (OR PHRASE) IN EACH SPEECH BUBBLE TO EMPHASIZE. UNDERLINE, ITALICIZE, OR MAKE THE WORD BOLD TO GIVE IT MORE ATTENTION.

COMIC #1

PEANUT...DO YOU THINK I SHOULD TELL DOT HOW I REALLY FEEL ABOUT HER?

WHAT?! OF COURSE YOU SHOULD, BRAMBLE.

IT'S JUST THAT... WELL...I'M NERVOUS.

YEAH, BUT YOU HAVE TO TELL HER.

I WOULDN'T HAVE THIS PROBLEM, IF DOT WASN'T SO CUTE!

COMIC #2

HEY, BRAMBLE!

OH--HEY, DOT! I WAS JUST... UM...YOU KNOW... I MEAN...I... UH.....

PEANUT SAID YOU HAVE SOMETHING TO TELL ME?

HE DID? I MEAN, I DO, BUT ...

BRAMBLE? ARE YOU OK?

UH

UM

UM

YOUR TURN!

CHOOSE YOUR OWN COMIC

CAN I CHOOSE ALL THE COMICS?

START READING THE COMIC BELOW. FOLLOW THE ARROWS TO KEEP GOING. WHEN YOU COME TO A PANEL WITH TWO ARROWS, PICK A DIRECTION AND KEEP READING!

THIS IS A CHOOSE-YOUR-OWN-COMIC MINI COMIC!

FOLLOW THE ARROWS TO KEEP READING. IF YOU REACH TWO ARROWS...

...PICK A DIRECTION AND KEEP READING!

SOME ARROWS CAN LEAD YOU TO AN END.

THE END.

STING !!! THE END. BUZZ

BUZZ!

SOME ARROWS KEEP THE COMIC GOING. HI, BEE!

THE END.

DO YOU THINK YOU COULD EVER CHOOSE BETWEEN TWO ENDINGS?

...I JUST WANT YOUR HONEY!

LOOK, BEE--I DON'T WANT ANY TROUBLE...

OF COURSE! THE END.

DO YOU THINK WE'LL ALWAYS BE FRIENDS?

I WAS JUST WONDERING... YEAH?

OH, HELLO BEES. PHEW!

...I'M JUST HERE FOR THE COMIC.

WHAT WERE WE DOING AGAIN? UGH.

OH YEAH--PICKING A DIRECTION!

Y'KNOW, BRAM...

WANNA SIT DOWN? YEAH! UNDER THAT TREE.

...IT'S MAKING ME HUNGRY.

BOY...ALL THIS WALKING...

GOOD CHOICE, BRAMBLE. THANKS!

...I LIKE CHOOSING COMICS! THE END.

  MOST AMERICAN COMICS ARE MEANT TO BE READ AS YOU WOULD A PAGE OF TEXT: FROM LEFT TO RIGHT, AND FROM TOP TO BOTTOM. HOWEVER, COMICS CAN USE WORDS, PICTURES, AND SYMBOLS TO GUIDE THE READER'S EYE THROUGH THE PAGE IN UNIQUE WAYS, CREATING A ONE-OF-A-KIND READING EXPERIENCE!

54

MAKE YOUR OWN... ...CHOOSE-YOUR-OWN-COMIC

STARTING IN THE TOP-LEFT PANEL, BEGIN MAKING A COMIC WITH BRANCHING STORYLINES. (IT MIGHT HELP TO CREATE ONE STORYLINE ALL THE WAY THROUGH, THEN GO BACK AND ADD TO THE STORY WHERE PANELS CONTAIN TWO ARROWS.)

BONUS: CREATE A "BOOK" VERSION OF YOUR COMIC BY RECREATING EACH PANEL AS ITS OWN PAGE. NUMBER YOUR PAGES, AND THEN TELL YOUR READERS WHERE TO TURN!

FOUR-PANEL CHALLENGE

WE ACCEPT!

PICK JUST FOUR PANELS FROM THE COMIC BELOW TO TELL THE ENTIRE STORY. USING A BRUSH AND/OR PEN, INK THE FOUR PANELS YOU CHOOSE TO KEEP.

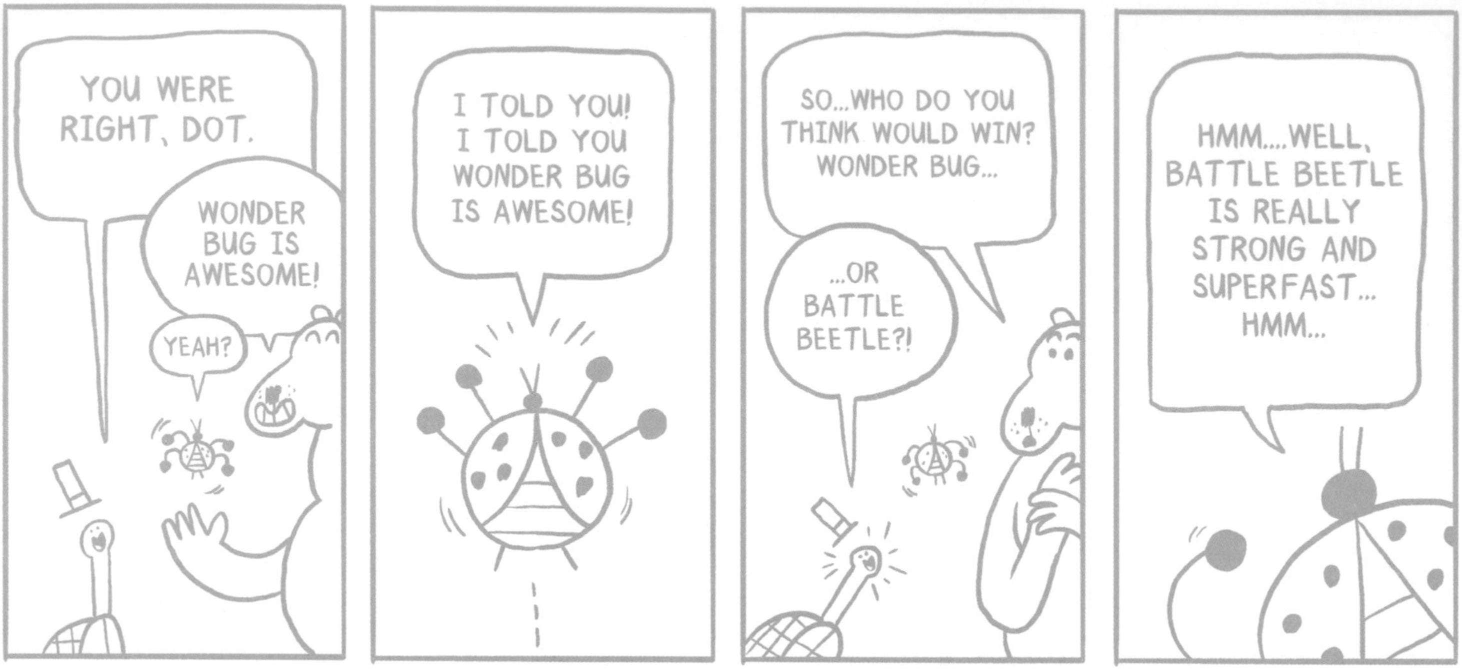

YOU WERE RIGHT, DOT.
WONDER BUG IS AWESOME!
YEAH?
I TOLD YOU! I TOLD YOU WONDER BUG IS AWESOME!
SO...WHO DO YOU THINK WOULD WIN? WONDER BUG...
...OR BATTLE BEETLE?!
HMM....WELL, BATTLE BEETLE IS REALLY STRONG AND SUPERFAST... HMM...

WHEN INKING YOUR COMIC, THINK ABOUT WHICH PARTS OF YOUR DRAWING WILL BE COMPLETELY FILLED WITH INK AND WHICH PARTS WILL APPEAR AS LINE ART.

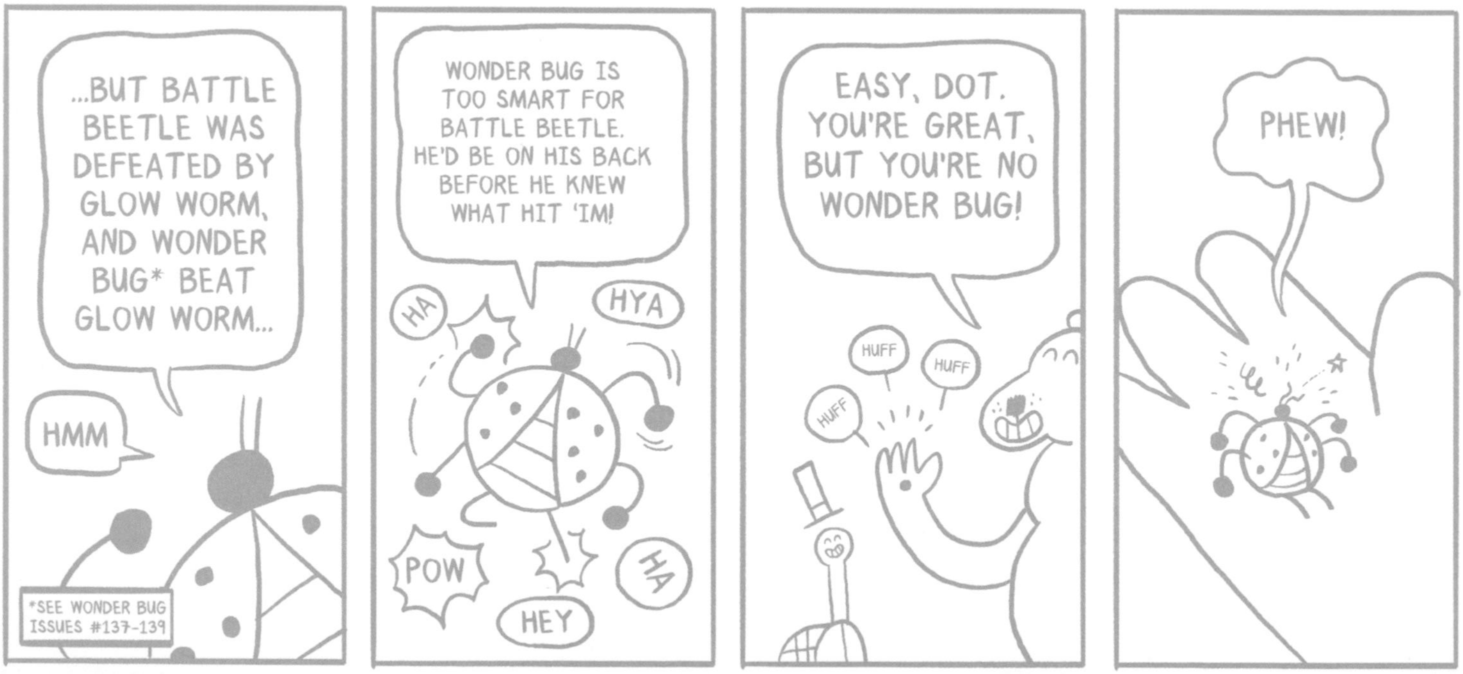

...BUT BATTLE BEETLE WAS DEFEATED BY GLOW WORM, AND WONDER BUG* BEAT GLOW WORM...
HMM
*SEE WONDER BUG ISSUES #137-139
WONDER BUG IS TOO SMART FOR BATTLE BEETLE. HE'D BE ON HIS BACK BEFORE HE KNEW WHAT HIT 'IM!
HA
HYA
POW
HA
HEY
EASY, DOT. YOU'RE GREAT, BUT YOU'RE NO WONDER BUG!
HUFF
HUFF
HUFF
PHEW!

PICKING WHICH PANELS TO KEEP AND WHICH TO THROW OUT IS AN IMPORTANT PART OF MAKING A COMIC. INCLUDING TWO PANELS THAT SAY THE SAME THING OR KEEPING A PANEL THAT DOESN'T ADD TO THE STORY CAN TAKE AWAY FROM THE MOST EXCITING AND IMPORTANT PARTS.

PICK AND INK

1 PICK ONE PANEL FROM EACH ROW BY INKING IT WITH A BRUSH OR PEN.

2 COPY THIS PAGE, CUT IT UP, AND GLUE YOUR PANELS IN ORDER TO COMPLETE YOUR COMIC!

FINISHED COMIC
→

PANEL 1 GOES HERE

PANEL 2 GOES HERE

PANEL 3 GOES HERE

THIS ROW IS THE BEGINNING OF THE COMIC. PICK YOUR FAVORITE PANEL AND INK IT.
→

PICK ONE PANEL FROM THIS ROW TO INK AND USE IT AS PANEL 2 IN YOUR FINAL COMIC, ABOVE.
→

PICK ONE PANEL FROM THIS ROW TO BE USED AS YOUR THIRD PANEL.
→

(REMEMBER TO CHOOSE A PANEL THAT DOES THE BEST JOB OF SHOWING HOW THE COMIC ENDS.)

 BONUS: CAN YOU INK THE REMAINING PANELS? TRY TO USE A BRUSH, PEN, OR MARKER THAT YOU WOULDN'T NORMALLY USE, AND THEN EXPLORE THE LINES MADE WITH WHATEVER TOOL YOU SELECT.

AGAIN AND AGAIN
 AGAIN?

THESE COMICS GO ON AND ON AND ON....THE END OF EACH COMIC CONTINUES BY GOING BACK TO THE FIRST PANEL, WHERE THE COMIC STARTS ALL OVER AGAIN. MAKE YOUR OWN LOOPING COMIC BELOW!

GO BACK TO PANEL 1

YUM!

-CLIMB-
-CLIMB-

I SMELL HONEY!

JACKPOT!

GO BACK TO PANEL 1

 BONUS: CAN YOU COME UP WITH A LOOPING CONVERSATION TO INCLUDE IN YOUR COMIC? ARE THERE OTHER WAYS THAT COMICS CAN LOOP, OR START OVER?

58

SUPER-SMART BEAR

BY

BRAMBLE

~~THERE ONCE WAS~~
ONCE upon
A time
All the
Bad Guys
~~In~~ ~~it~~
🍯 stole
the Honey.

But, A Brave
~~cub~~ Bear Named
Bramble
Ate some of
🍯 the Honey

~~Then~~ And Turned
Into
Super-Smart ~~Bear~~!

YUM

And That Is ~~He~~
How He Became
Super-Smart Bear.

↑ Honey Beard

Super-Smart Bear
Caught The Bad
Guys.

Help!
We're
STUCK
In
Honey!

You're STUCK
Now!

Super-Smart Bear saved the children.

"Ha! Ha!"

"You saved Me!!"

"You're welcome."

And Memorized the Numbers ALL the WAY up to ONE hunndred!!

1, 2, 3, 4, 5, 6, 7, 8, 9, 10, 11, 12, 13, 14, 15, 16, 17, 18, 19, 20, 21, 22, 23, 24, 25, 26, 27, 28, 29, 30, 31, 32, 33, 34, 35, 36, 37, 38, 39, 40, 41, 42, 43, 44, 45, 46, 47, 48, 49, 50, 51, 52, 53, 54, 55, 56, 57, 58, 59, 60, 61, 62, 63, 64, 65, 66, 67, 68, 69, 70, 71, 72, 73, 74, 75, 76, 77, 78, 79, 80, 81, 82, 83, 84, 85, 86, 87, 88, 89, 90, 91, 92, 93, 94, 95, 96, 97, 98, 99, 100!!

But One Guy Thought that Super-Smart BEAR Couldn't Say the Numbers Backwards, But He Could

100, 99, 98, 97, 96, 95, 94, 93, 92, 91, 90, 89, 88, 87, 86, 85, 84, 83, 82, 81, 80, 79, 78, 77, 76, 75, 74, 73, 72, 71, 70, 69, 68, 67, 66, 65, 64, 63, 62, 61, 60, 59, 58, 57, 56, 55, 54, 53, 52, 51, 50, 49, 48, 47, 46, 45, 44, 43, 42, 41, 40, 39, 38, 37, 36, 35, 34, 33, 32, 31, 30, 29, 28, 27, 26, 25, 24, 23, 22, 21, 20, 19, 18, 17, 16, 15, 14, 13, 12, 11, 10, 9, 8, 7, 6, 5, 4, 3, 2, 1!!!!!!!!

Then, All the Honey was Gone, But ~~Bramble~~ SUPER-SMART BEAR Had the Bees Make More, so There was More Honey

"OK"

Super-Smart Bear Is Really BRAMBLE!

BY Bramble

A.K.A. Super-Smart Bear

THREE-PANEL CHALLENGE

I, SUPER-SMART BEAR, CHALLENGE YOU TO CONDENSE THE NEXT SIX PANELS INTO ONLY THREE PANELS ON A NEW SHEET OF PAPER! INCLUDE ALL THE IMPORTANT PARTS--AND ONLY USE THREE PANELS! I BELIEVE IN YOU!

DO WHAT ~~BRAMBLE~~ SUPER-SMART BEAR SAYS.

CUTTING YOUR COMIC TO INCLUDE ONLY THE MOST IMPORTANT PARTS KEEPS YOUR STORY MOVING FORWARD AND KEEPS THE READER INTERESTED.

WELCOME TO THE WORLD-FAMOUS--

PEN OLYMPICS!

MAKE COPIES OF THIS PAGE FOR EVERYONE PLAYING. THE GOAL IS TO USE A BRUSH OR PEN TO TRACE THE WANDERING LINE AS CLOSELY AS POSSIBLE. THE FIRST ONE TO FINISH WINS!

ON YOUR MARK...

GET SET...

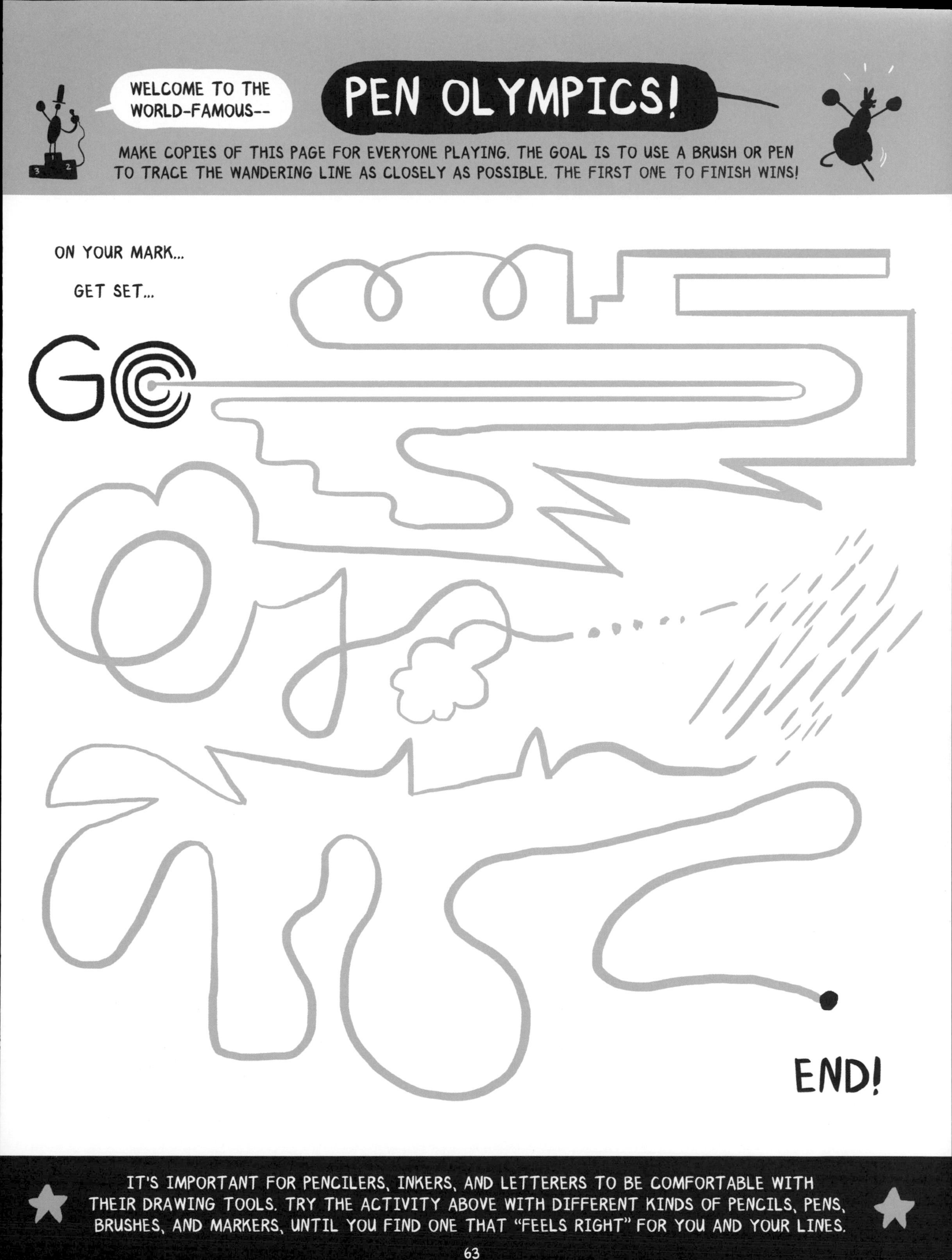
GO
END!

IT'S IMPORTANT FOR PENCILERS, INKERS, AND LETTERERS TO BE COMFORTABLE WITH THEIR DRAWING TOOLS. TRY THE ACTIVITY ABOVE WITH DIFFERENT KINDS OF PENCILS, PENS, BRUSHES, AND MARKERS, UNTIL YOU FIND ONE THAT "FEELS RIGHT" FOR YOU AND YOUR LINES.

MATCHY-MATCH

MATCHY-MATCH!

HOW WELL DO YOU KNOW YOUR COMICS TERMS? MATCH EACH TERM WITH ITS DEFINITION. (HINT: SOME ANSWERS ARE IN THE GLOSSARY ON PAGE 88!)

HEY...WE MATCH!

EMANATA

SPEECH BUBBLE

ONOMATOPOEIA

SUDDENLY...

BEE

POW!

PANEL

THOUGHT BALLOON

CAPTION

MOTION LINES

UNDERSTANDING COMICS TERMS ALLOWS DIFFERENT COMICS CREATORS TO CLEARLY IDENTIFY PARTS OF COMICS, WHETHER THEY BE ACTION, ALTERNATIVE, COMIC STRIPS, DIGITAL, GRAPHIC NOVELS, HUMOR, MANGA, OR OTHER KINDS OF COMICS.

HALF OF THIS COMIC HAS ALREADY BEEN MADE, BUT YOU'LL NEED TO COME UP WITH A LIST OF WORDS TO COMPLETE THE OTHER HALF!

FOOD:
_____

TEMPERATURE:
_____

SEASON:
_____

NOUN:
_____

ADJECTIVE:
_____

SPORT:
_____

ROOM IN BUILDING:
_____

FOOD:
_____

EXPENSIVE OBJECTS:
_____

ACTIVITY ENDING IN 'ING':
_____

SPECIFIC PLACE:
_____

NUMBER:
_____

DEAR DOT...
THIS IS BRAMBLE. (REMEMBER-- THE BEAR?) I WANTED TO WRITE AND TELL YOU THAT YOU SMELL LIKE _____ ON A _____
(FOOD)   (TEMPERATURE)
_____ DAY. YOU REMIND ME
(SEASON)
OF A _____ , JUST
(NOUN)
AFTER THE RAIN.

HAVE YOU SEEN THE MOVIE
_____ _____ ?
(ADJECTIVE)   (SPORT)
I HAVE A COPY IN MY
_____ .
(ROOM IN A BUILDING)
WE COULD WATCH IT TOGETHER SOMETIME. I COULD EVEN MAKE
_____ .
(FOOD)

YOUR EYES ARE LIKE
_____
(EXPENSIVE OBJECTS)
AND I HOPE ONE DAY WE CAN GO _____
(ACTIVITY ENDING IN 'ING')
OR TAKE A TRIP TO
_____
(SPECIFIC PLACE)
I'VE SAVED UP $ _____ .
(NUMBER)
I'M TRYING TO TELL YOU I LIKE YOU.

DO YOU LIKE ME?

BRAMBLE

ASSEMBLE PEANUT & BRAMBLE'S
"PET PROBLEM"!

I'M BASICALLY FAMOUS!

 1 CAREFULLY REMOVE THE NEXT FOUR PAGES FROM THIS BOOK.

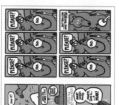

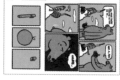

2 PLACE YOUR PAGES IN THE FOLLOWING ORDER:

TOP →

BOTTOM →

3 FOLD YOUR PAGES IN HALF, FOLDING LEFT TO RIGHT.

IT'S ME-- I'M FAMOUS!

4 ENJOY YOUR VERY OWN PEANUT & BRAMBLE COMIC!

MY NEW FAVORITE COMIC!

I'M SO FAMOUS!

MAKING COPIES OF PEANUT & BRAMBLE'S "PET PROBLEM" IS EASY. SIMPLY COPY EACH PAGE TO A NEW SHEET OF PAPER AND FOLLOW STEPS 2-4.

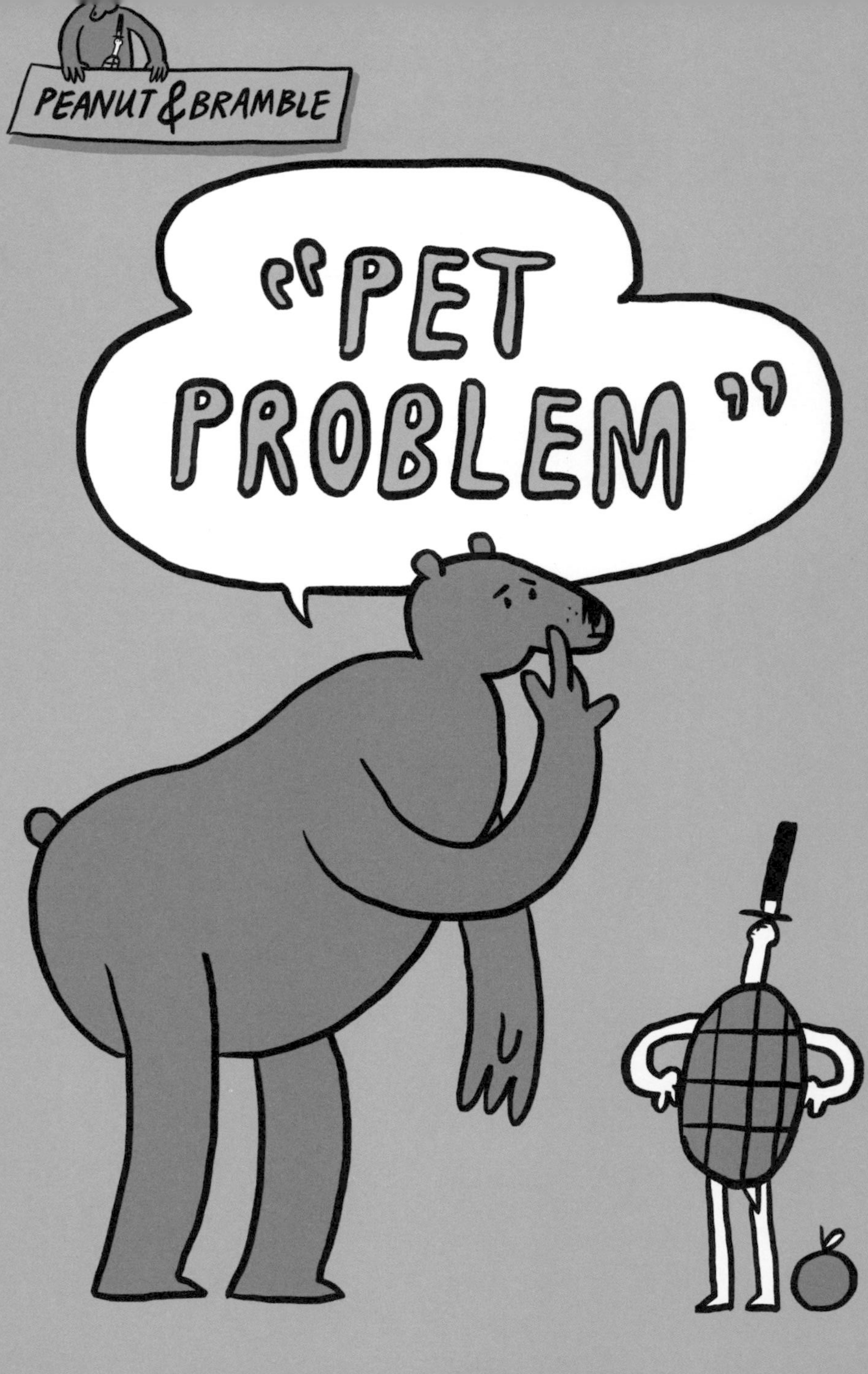
PEANUT & BRAMBLE
"PET PROBLEM"

JESS SMART SMILEY

PEANUT & BRAMBLE

#PEANUTBRAMBLE

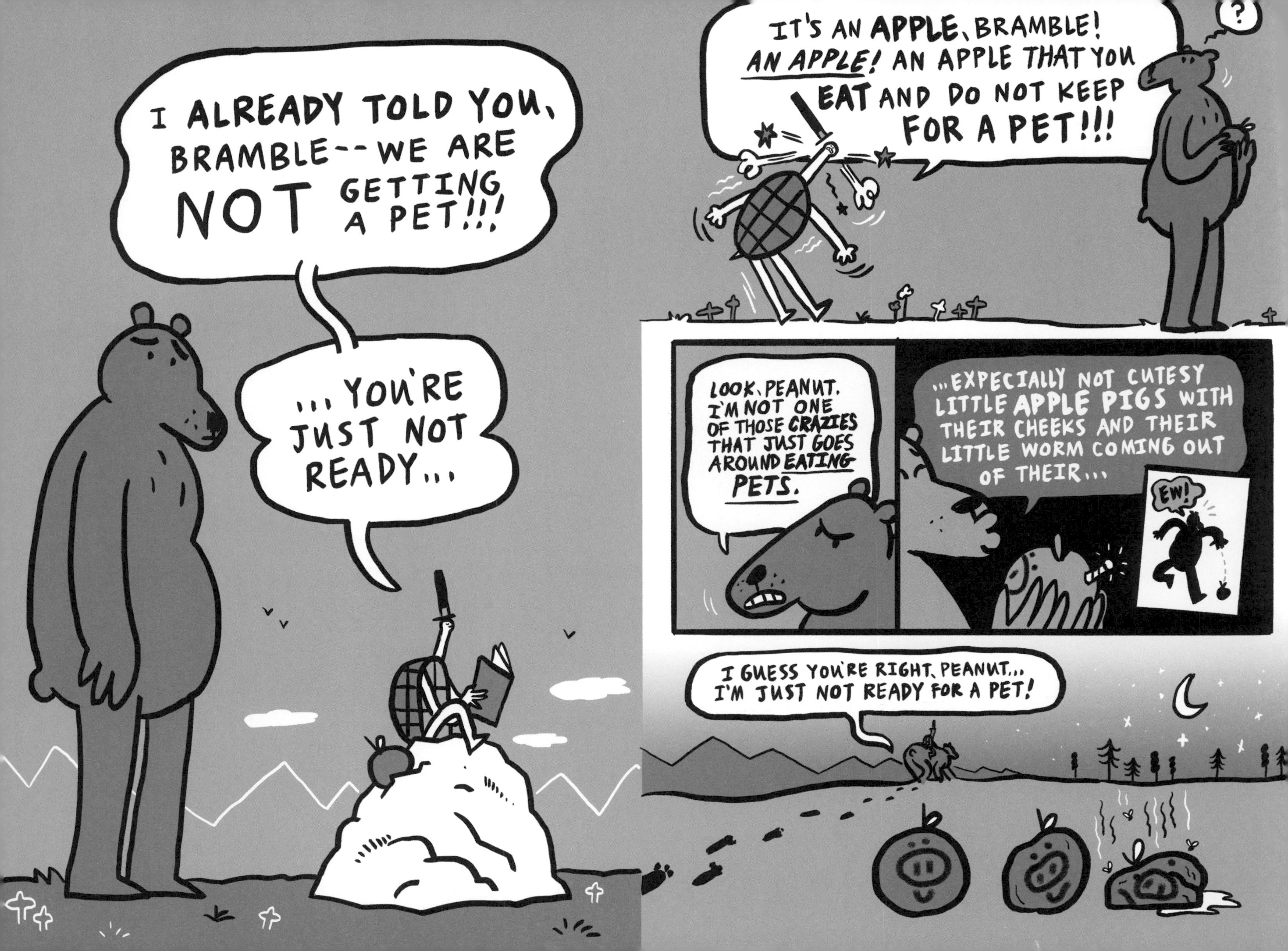
I ALREADY TOLD YOU, BRAMBLE--WE ARE NOT GETTING A PET!!!
... YOU'RE JUST NOT READY...
IT'S AN APPLE, BRAMBLE! AN APPLE! AN APPLE THAT YOU EAT AND DO NOT KEEP FOR A PET!!!
?
LOOK, PEANUT. I'M NOT ONE OF THOSE CRAZIES THAT JUST GOES AROUND EATING PETS.
...EXPECIALLY NOT CUTESY LITTLE APPLE PIGS WITH THEIR CHEEKS AND THEIR LITTLE WORM COMING OUT OF THEIR...
EW!
I GUESS YOU'RE RIGHT, PEANUT... I'M JUST NOT READY FOR A PET!

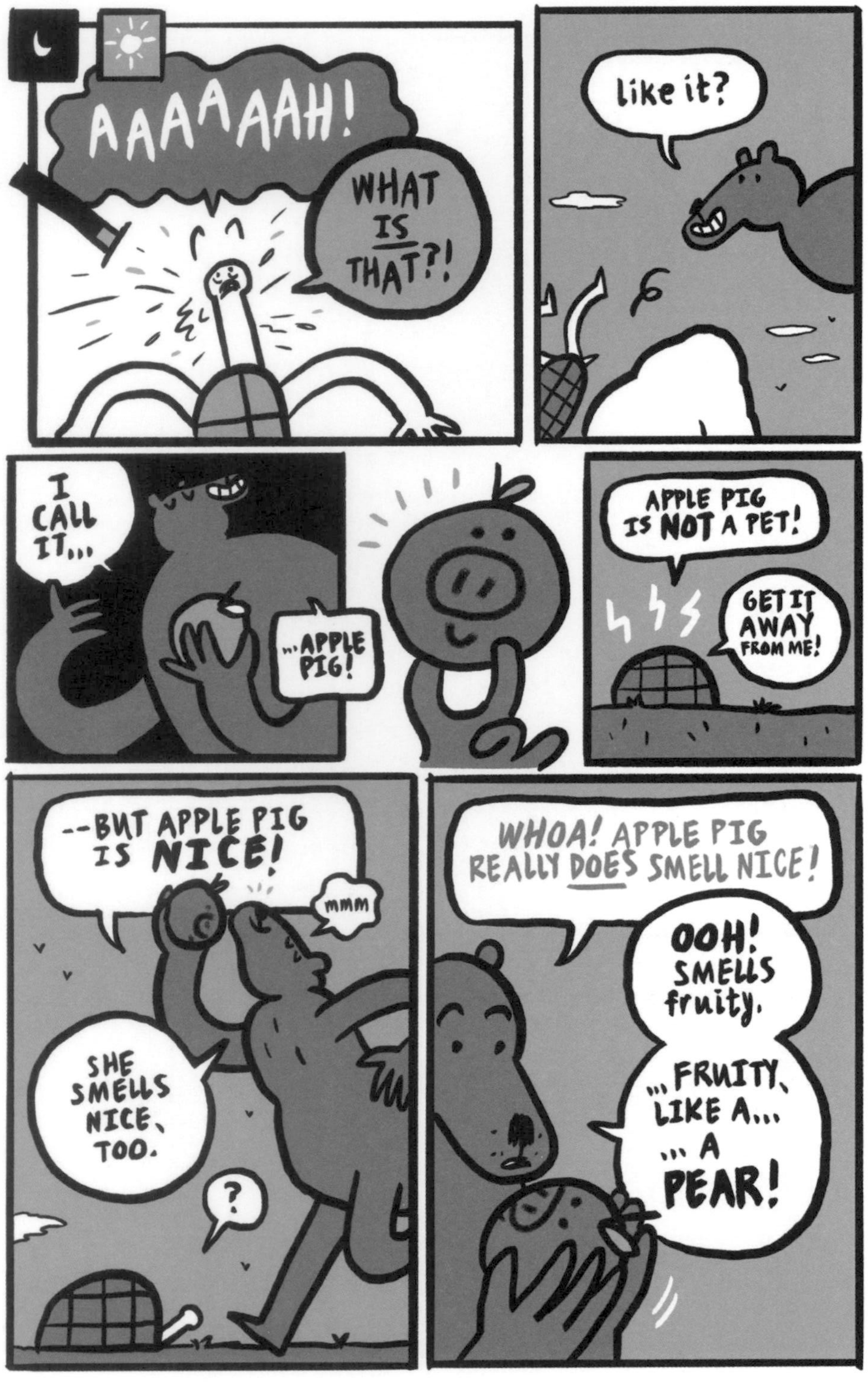
AAAAAAH!
WHAT IS THAT?!
like it?
I CALL IT...
...APPLE PIG!
APPLE PIG IS NOT A PET!
GET IT AWAY FROM ME!
--BUT APPLE PIG IS NICE!
mmm
SHE SMELLS NICE, TOO.
?
WHOA! APPLE PIG REALLY DOES SMELL NICE!
OOH! SMELLS fruity.
...FRUITY, LIKE A... ...A PEAR!

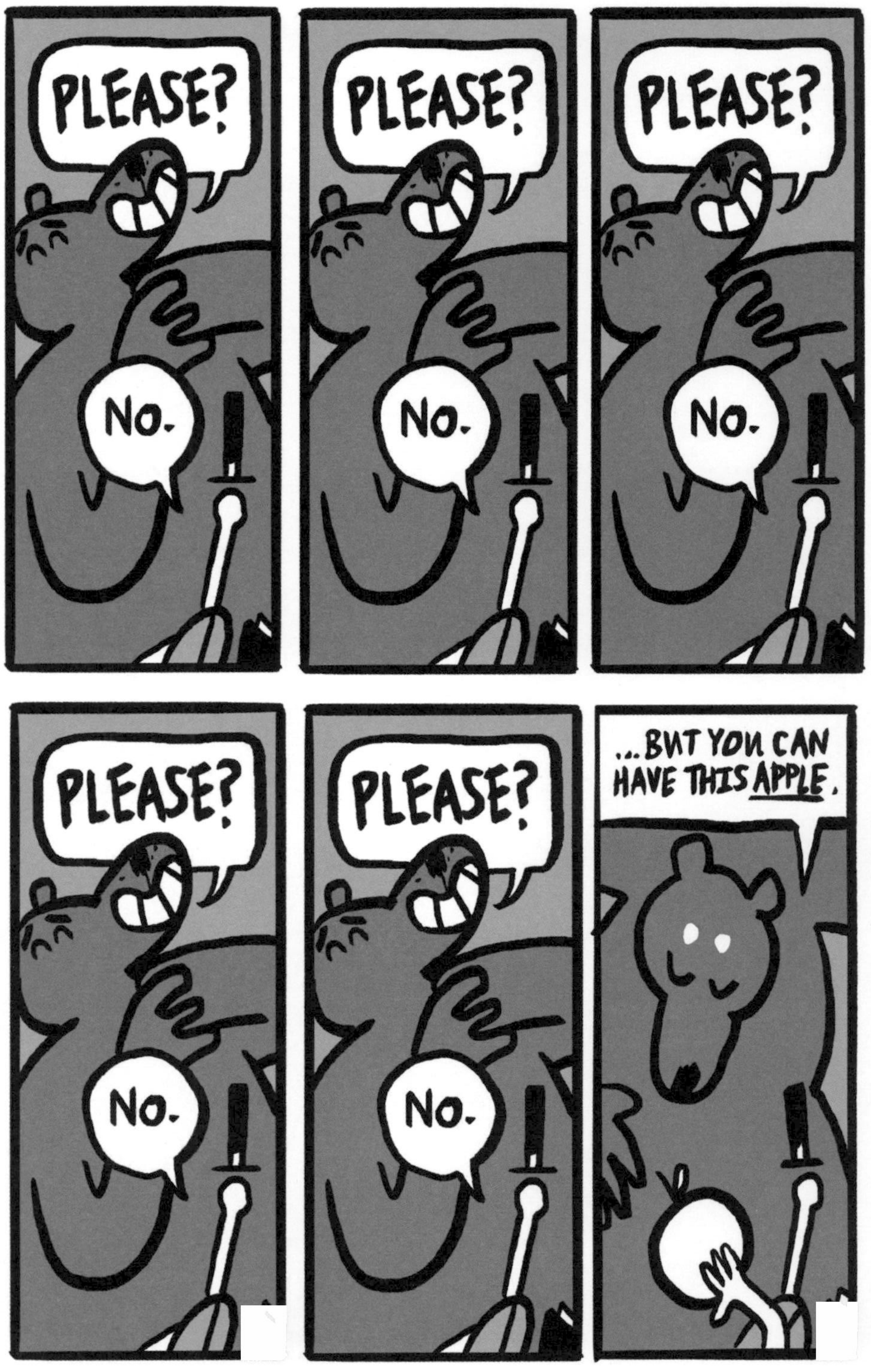
PLEASE?
No.
PLEASE?
No.
PLEASE?
No.
PLEASE?
No.
PLEASE?
No.
...BUT YOU CAN HAVE THIS APPLE.

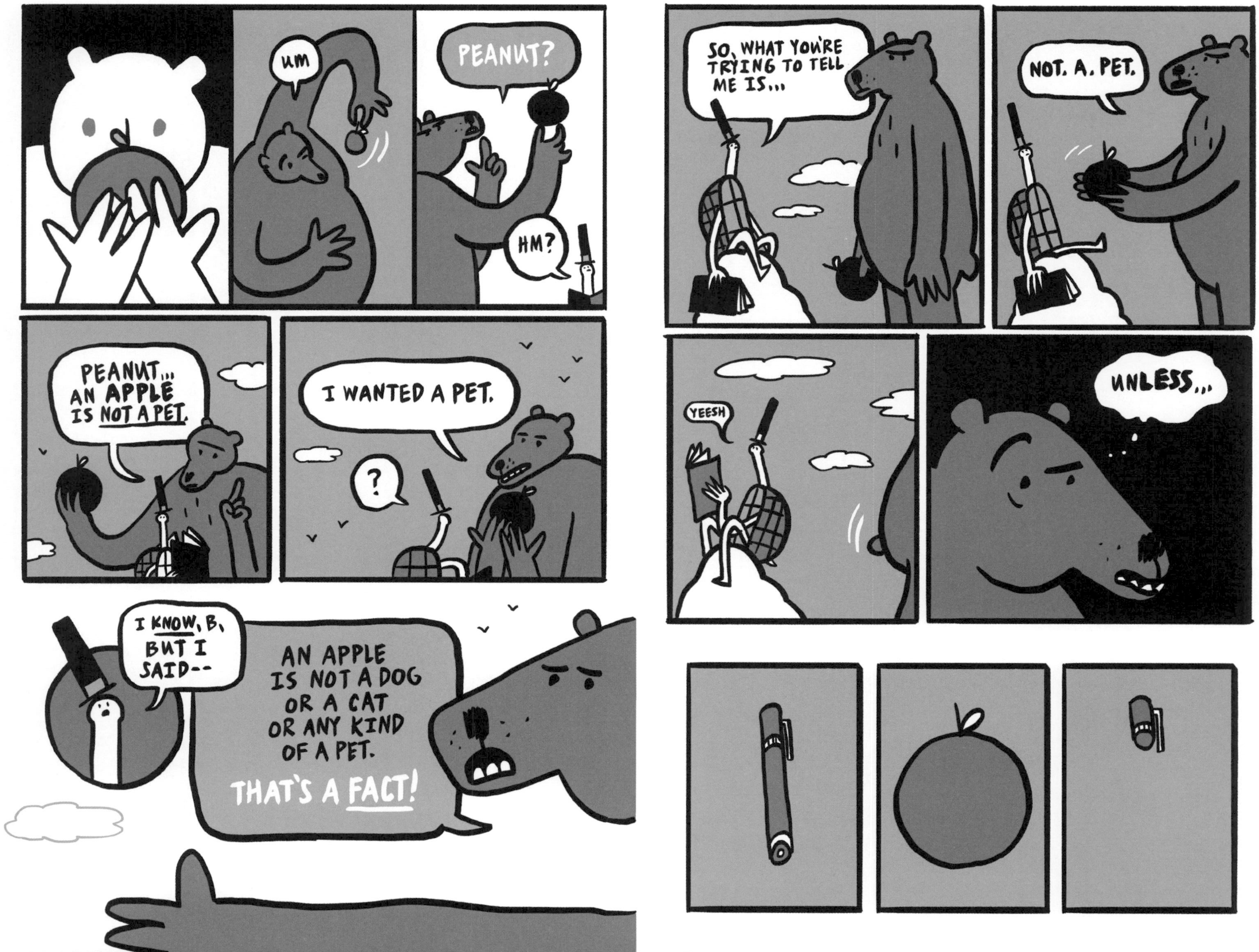

UM
PEANUT?
HM?
PEANUT... AN APPLE IS NOT A PET.
I WANTED A PET.
?
I KNOW, B, BUT I SAID--
AN APPLE IS NOT A DOG OR A CAT OR ANY KIND OF A PET.
THAT'S A FACT!
SO, WHAT YOU'RE TRYING TO TELL ME IS...
NOT. A. PET.
YEESH
UNLESS...

TO MAKE THIS COMIC, YOU WILL NEED:

paper • a pencil • a pen or marker • scissors

LET'S MAKE AN EIGHT-PAGE MINI COMIC!

BY PEANUT

FRONT

1

2 FOLD

FOLD 1

3 FOLD

2

UNFOLD AND NUMBER PAGES

BACK | FRONT | 1 | 2
3 | 4 | 5 | 6

3

CUT ALONG DOTTED LINE IN CENTER

BACK | FRONT | 1 | 2
3 | 4 | 5 | 6

4

FOLD, LIKE SO:

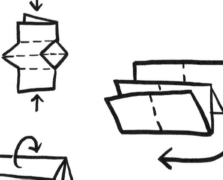

5

THINGS TO MAKE A COMIC ABOUT:

• YOUR PET
• A FAIRY TALE
• SCHOOL
• SWIMMING
• ALIENS
• FLYING
• COOKING

THAT'S IT!

BE SURE TO MAKE COPIES FOR YOUR FRIENDS AND FAMILY AND EVEN SHARE IT ONLINE.

6

UNFOLD YOUR COMIC ALL THE WAY TO MAKE COPIES OF IT.

THE END

BACK

PAUSE

WHY, YES--I DID JUST WASH MY PAWS...

...THANK YOU FOR NOTICING!

WHICH DRAMATIC PAUSE WORKS BEST IN THE COMIC BELOW?
PICK YOUR FAVORITE, AND THEN INK IT WITH A BRUSH OR A PEN.

A PERFECTLY PLACED PAUSE CAN ADD HUMOR, DRAMA, SUSPENSE, AND MORE. PAY ATTENTION TO
THE NEXT COMIC YOU READ AND WATCH FOR THE PAUSES. HOW DO THEY ADD TO THE STORY?

FOLLOW THE SCRIPT!
PART 1

LET'S DO THIS!

USE THE SCRIPT BELOW TO MAKE YOUR OWN PEANUT & BRAMBLE COMIC ON THE NEXT PAGE.
BE SURE TO USE THE DIALOGUE FROM THE SCRIPT AND ALSO DRAW WHAT IS DESCRIBED.

"THE REAL SUPERHEROES"

ILLUSTRATED BY _____

USE THIS AREA TO WRITE
OR DRAW ANY ADDITIONAL
IDEAS YOU HAVE.

PANEL 1
PEANUT & BRAMBLE ARE WALKING UP A HILL,
READING COMICS. THE SUN IS OUT. WE SEE
MOUNTAINS IN THE DISTANCE.

PANEL 2
CLOSE-UP OF BRAMBLE.
    BRAMBLE: HEY, PEANUT...DO YOU THINK
    THERE ARE ANY REAL SUPERHEROES?

PANEL 3
PEANUT LOOKS CONFUSED AND STOPS WALKING.
    PEANUT: YOU MEAN REAL PEOPLE
    WITH REAL SUPERPOWERS?
    BRAMBLE: YEAH!

PANEL 4
    PEANUT: DOES MAGIC COUNT AS A
    SUPERPOWER?
BRAMBLE LOOKS HUNGRY.
    BRAMBLE: CAN YOU MAGIC ME SOME
    HONEY RIGHT NOW?

PANEL 5
PEANUT SEES A BEEHIVE AND GETS EXCITED.
BRAMBLE WONDERS WHY PEANUT IS EXCITED.

PANEL 6
PEANUT PRETENDS TO MAKE THE BEEHIVE
APPEAR BEHIND BRAMBLE.
    PEANUT: MAGIC!
BRAMBLE GOBBLES THE HONEY.
    BRAMBLE: I KNEW IT! SUPERPOWERS
    ARE REAL!

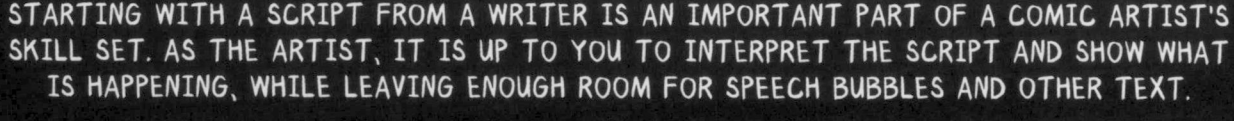

STARTING WITH A SCRIPT FROM A WRITER IS AN IMPORTANT PART OF A COMIC ARTIST'S
SKILL SET. AS THE ARTIST, IT IS UP TO YOU TO INTERPRET THE SCRIPT AND SHOW WHAT
IS HAPPENING, WHILE LEAVING ENOUGH ROOM FOR SPEECH BUBBLES AND OTHER TEXT.

BONUS: INVITE YOUR FRIENDS TO DRAW THEIR OWN PEANUT & BRAMBLE COMIC USING "THE REAL SUPERHEROES" SCRIPT. DO YOUR COMICS LOOK THE SAME? WHAT'S DIFFERENT ABOUT THEM?

FOLLOW THE SCRIPT

PART 2

FOLLOWING THE SCRIPT ON THE PREVIOUS PAGE, CREATE YOUR "REAL SUPERHEROES" COMIC BELOW. USE A PENCIL TO LIGHTLY DRAW YOUR COMIC BEFORE INKING IT.

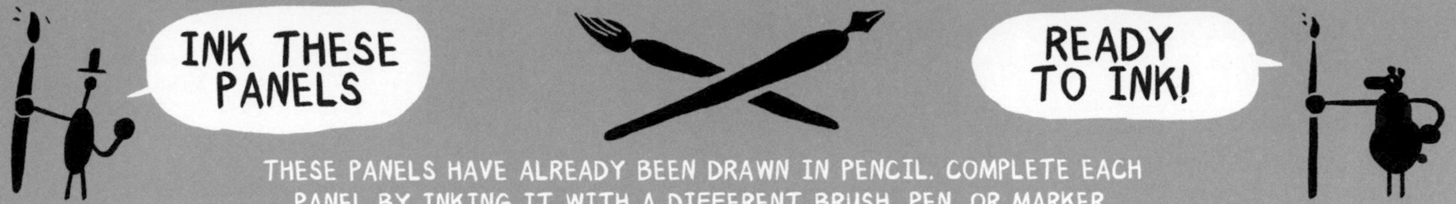
INK THESE PANELS
READY TO INK!

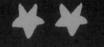

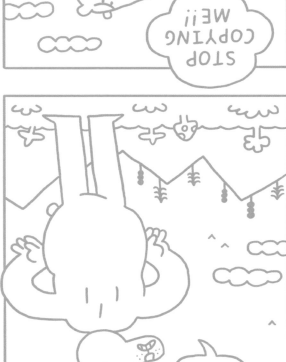

THESE PANELS HAVE ALREADY BEEN DRAWN IN PENCIL. COMPLETE EACH PANEL BY INKING IT WITH A DIFFERENT BRUSH, PEN, OR MARKER.

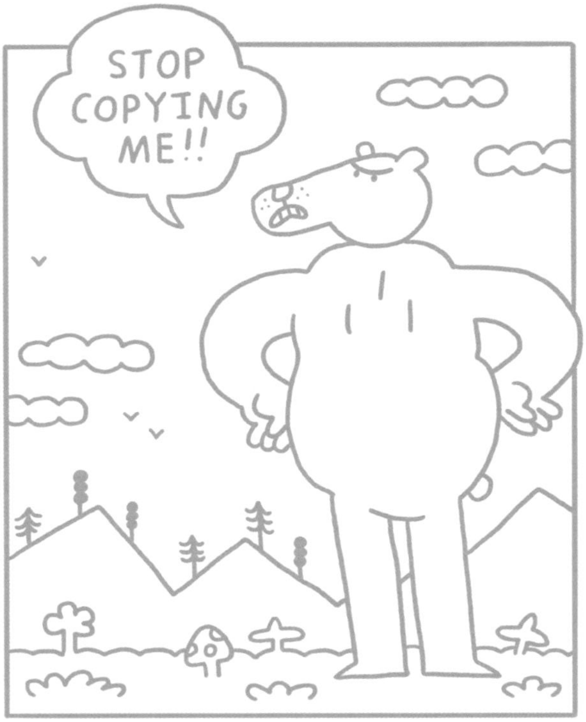
STOP COPYING ME!!

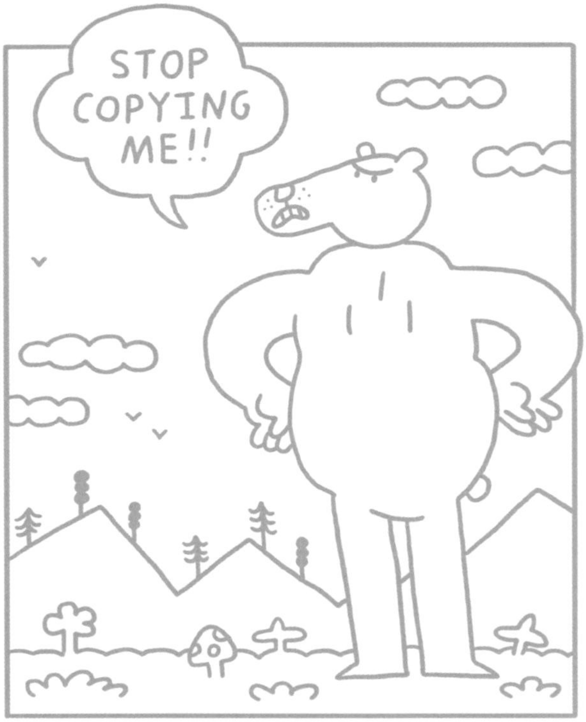
STOP COPYING ME!!

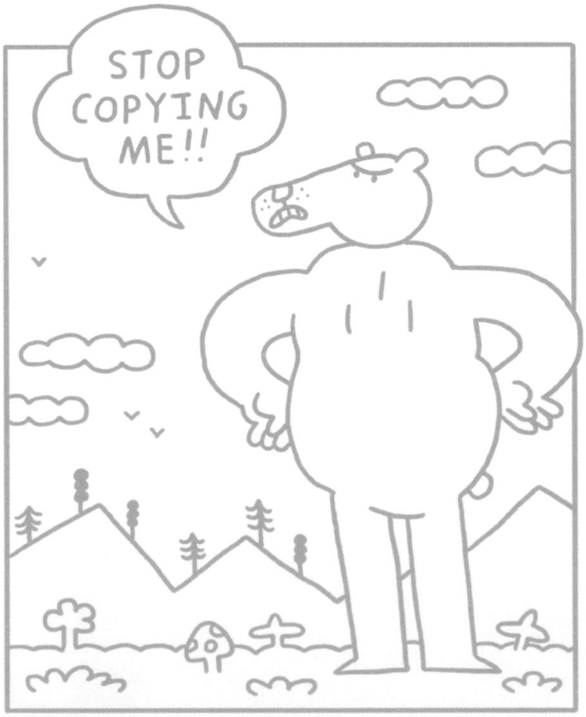
STOP COPYING ME!!

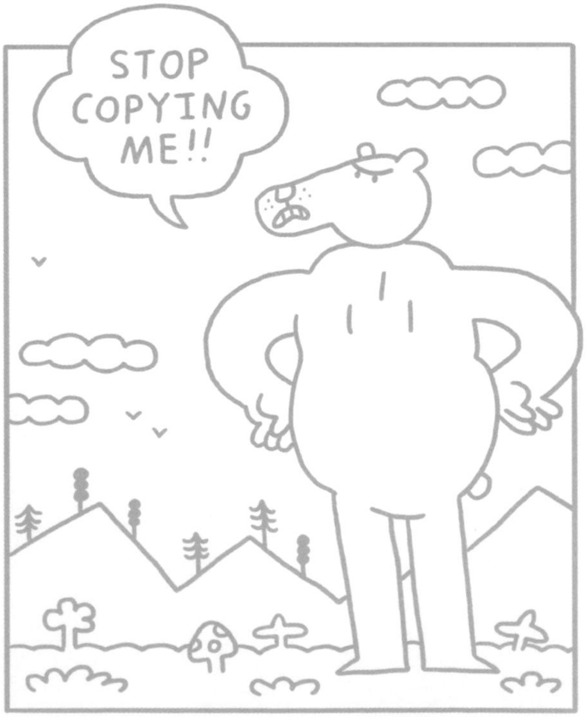
STOP COPYING ME!!

INKING IS AN IMPORTANT PART OF THE COMICS-MAKING PROCESS. DARK LINES HELP THE READER SEE THE CHARACTERS, BACKGROUNDS, AND WORDS CLEARLY SO THAT THE STORY MAKES SENSE.

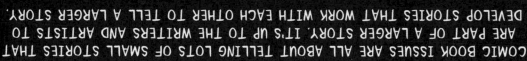

COMICS CROSSWORD

ARE YOU SURE THIS'LL WORK?

FINISH THE CROSSWORD BELOW BY COMPLETING THE CHALLENGE FOR EACH ROW AND COLUMN. TRY TO MAKE EACH STORYLINE CONNECT.

COMIC BOOK ISSUES ARE ALL ABOUT TELLING LOTS OF SMALL STORIES THAT ARE PART OF A LARGER STORY. IT'S UP TO THE WRITERS AND ARTISTS TO DEVELOP STORIES THAT WORK WITH EACH OTHER TO TELL A LARGER STORY.

DOWN ↑

1 INCLUDE ONE THOUGHT BUBBLE.
3 INCLUDE A CLOCK.
5 INCLUDE THE SUN OR MOON.

ACROSS ←

2 INCLUDE ONE SOUND EFFECT (ONOMATOPOEIA).
4 INCLUDE ONE CLOSE-UP.

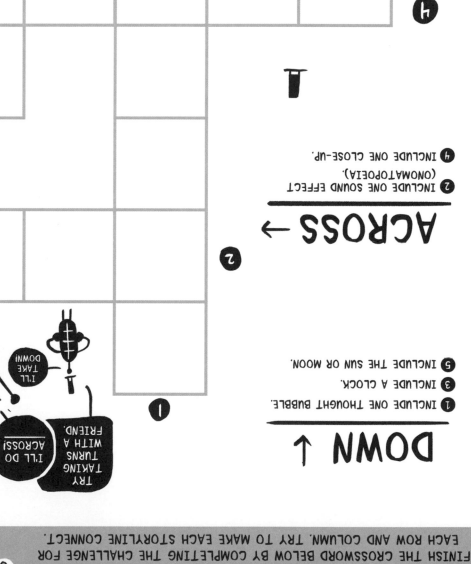

KEEP THINGS SIMPLE.

STICK FIGURES ARE GREAT!

TRY TAKING TURNS WITH A FRIEND.

I'LL DO ACROSS!

I'LL TAKE DOWN!

LET'S GO LINE-DANCING

YEE-HAW!

ROUND UP A PEN, BRUSH, AND INK, AND COMPLETE THE CHALLENGES BELOW!

USING YOUR PEN, MAKE A SERIES OF THIN LINES. DRAW THE LINES CLOSE TOGETHER, BUT DON'T LET THEM TOUCH!

LIKE THIS!

NOW DO THE SAME THING WITH YOUR BRUSH, BUT DON'T LET YOUR LINES TOUCH! TRY BOTH THICK AND THIN LINES.

I THINK I DREW A ZEBRA!

USING YOUR BRUSH, MAKE A THIN LINE THAT GETS THICKER, AND THEN DRAW A THICK LINE AND MAKE IT GET THINNER AS YOU GO.

THESE ARE SOME FINE LINES!

NOW DRAW TEN LINES, ALTERNATING THICK TO THIN, AND THIN TO THICK.

COOL!

CONTROLLING YOUR LINES MEANS CONTROLLING YOUR DRAWINGS. WHETHER YOU DRAW STICK FIGURES, CARTOONS, SUPERHEROES, OR SOMETHING MORE "REALISTIC," IT'S IMPORTANT TO KNOW WHAT YOUR PENS AND BRUSHES ARE CAPABLE OF AND HOW TO CONTROL THEM.

DIFFERENT--BUT THE SAME

CAN YOU USE THE SAME WORD (AND ONLY THAT WORD) TO TELL A COMPLETE STORY IN A SINGLE THREE-PANEL COMIC? LET'S FIND OUT BELOW!

THE ONLY WORD USED IN THIS COMIC IS...

YES.

MAKE YOUR OWN COMIC USING ONLY THE WORD...

GREAT.

NOW SELECT YOUR OWN WORD TO USE IN THIS COMIC...

COMICS ARE GREAT AT GETTING THE MOST OUT OF A FEW LINES, A FEW IMAGES, AND A FEW WORDS. THE ABILITY TO TELL A COMPLETE STORY USING A SINGLE WORD IS AN EXERCISE IN ECONOMY FOR ANY COMICS CREATOR.

84

CAN A COMIC STILL WORK WITHOUT PANEL BORDERS? HOW? CAN YOU FIND
EXAMPLES OF BORDERLESS PANELS IN SOME OF THE COMICS YOU'VE READ?

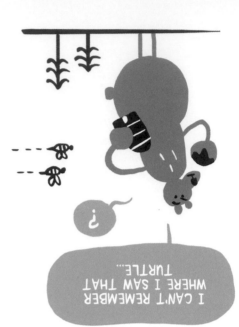

DO THICK OR THIN PANEL BORDERS WORK BEST? TRY MAKING A DECORATIVE BORDER USING DIFFERENT KINDS OF SHAPES.

WHERE ARE THE BORDERS?

OOPS! THIS COMIC IS MISSING PANEL BORDERS. COMPLETE THE
COMIC BY DRAWING PANEL BORDERS AROUND EACH PART OF THE COMIC.

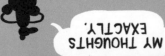

DOES THIS COMIC WORK BETTER IN TWO PANELS OR SIX? WHY? WHAT WOULD YOU
CHANGE ABOUT THE TWO- OR SIX-PANEL COMIC TO MAKE THE STORY EVEN BETTER?

YOUR TURN!
PRETEND BRAMBLE
IS MOVING IN
SLOW MOTION
IN THESE SIX PANELS.

SIX-PANEL CHALLENGE

BRING IT ON!

CAN YOU RECREATE THIS TWO-PANEL COMIC ABOUT BRAMBLE AS A SIX-PANEL COMIC?
SLOW THE STORY DOWN, THEN WRITE AND DRAW EACH MOMENT TO FILL ALL SIX PANELS.

OBSTACLE COURSE

PICK A CHARACTER (PEANUT, BRAMBLE, OR A CHARACTER OF YOUR OWN), AND HELP THE CHARACTER THROUGH THE OBSTACLE COURSE BELOW BY DRAWING THE CHARACTER COMPLETING EACH CHALLENGE. GOOD LUCK!

ON YOUR MARK...

GET SET

GO!

DRAW YOUR CHARACTER IN RUNNING STANCE, READY TO COMPETE.

IT'S A MAD DASH TO THE FIRST CHALLENGE!

DRAW YOUR CHARACTER JUMPING OVER THE CONE.

WE'LL SEE IF THE CONTESTANTS CAN SWING IT...

DRAW YOUR CHARACTER SWINGING ACROSS THIS PIT OF HUNGRY ALLIGATORS!

WE'RE ABOUT TO TAKE THIS TO THE NEXT LEVEL!

DRAW YOUR CHARACTER CLIMBING THIS DANGEROUS CLIFF.

IT'S A RACE TO THE FINISH!

DRAW YOUR CHARACTER RUNNING AS FAST AS THEY CAN.

WE HAVE A WINNER!

DRAW YOUR CHARACTER WITH THEIR WINNING TROPHY.

ONE OF THE BEST PARTS OF MAKING A COMIC IS DRAWING A CHARACTER THAT YOU LOVE IN ALL KINDS OF DIFFERENT POSITIONS AND IN ALL KINDS OF SITUATIONS. SHOWING YOUR CHARACTER IN ACTION MAKES THE CHARACTER MORE BELIEVABLE AND EXCITING TO YOUR READERS.

HOW TO MAKE...

"BRAMBLE'S LITTLE LAUGH BOOK"

FOLLOW THE DIRECTIONS BELOW TO ASSEMBLE YOUR OWN THIRTY-TWO-PAGE COMIC BOOK.

1 TEAR OUT THE NEXT PAGE FROM THIS BOOK.

PAGE 83

PAGE 84

FRONT

BACK

2 USING A COPIER, MAKE A DOUBLE-SIDED COPY OF THE PAGE.
(MAKE SURE BOTH SIDES ARE RIGHT-SIDE UP!)

COPY!

3 CAREFULLY CUT UP THE MIDDLE OF THE PAGE, DIVIDING IT IN HALF.

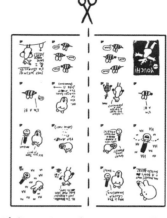

4 CUT ALONG EACH ROW AND ALIGN YOUR PAGES IN THIS ORDER:

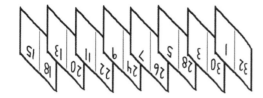

1 3 5 7 9 11 13 15
32 30 28 26 24 22 20 18

5 STAPLE IN THE CENTER AND FOLD YOUR BOOK IN HALF.

WOW!

MOM!

THIRTY-TWO PAGES FROM A SINGLE SHEET OF PAPER!

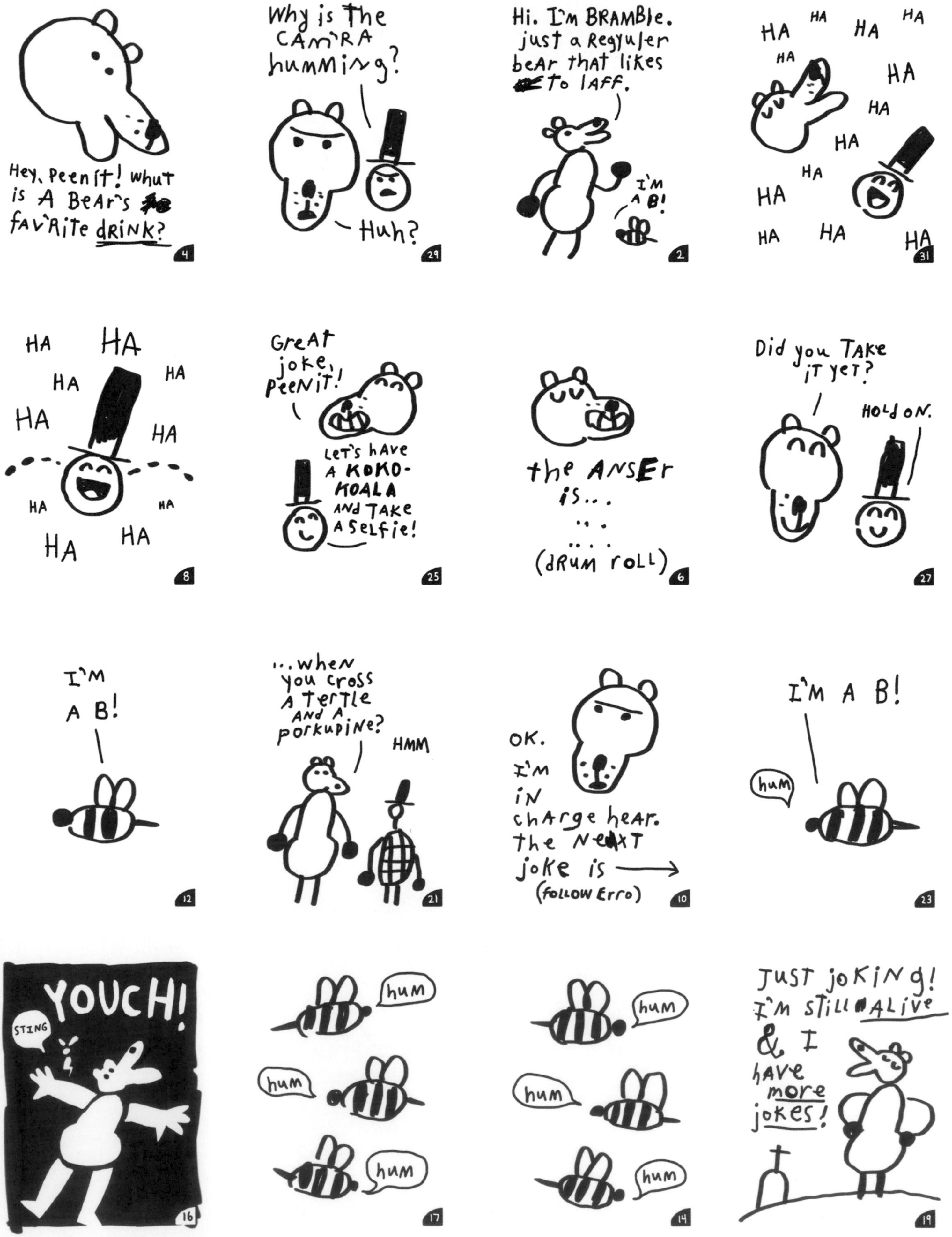
Hey, Peenit! whut is A Bear's favRite dRINK?
4
Why is The CAM'RA humming?
Huh?
29
Hi. I'm BRAMBle. just a Regyuler bear that likes To LAFF.
I'M A B!
2
HA HA HA HA HA HA HA HA HA HA HA HA
31
HA HA HA HA HA HA HA HA HA HA
8
Great joke, PeeNiT!
Let's hAve A KOKO-KOALA AND TAKE A Selfie!
25
the ANSEr is...
(dRUM roLL)
6
Did you TAKE iT yeT?
HOLd ON.
27
I'M A B!
12
...when you cross A Tertle AND A porkupiNe?
HMM
21
OK. I'm iN charge hear. the NEXT joke is
(FOLLOW Erro)
10
I'M A B!
hum
23
YOUCH!
STING
16
hum
hum
hum
17
hum
hum
hum
14
JUST joKiNg! I'M STILL ALive & I have more jokes!
19

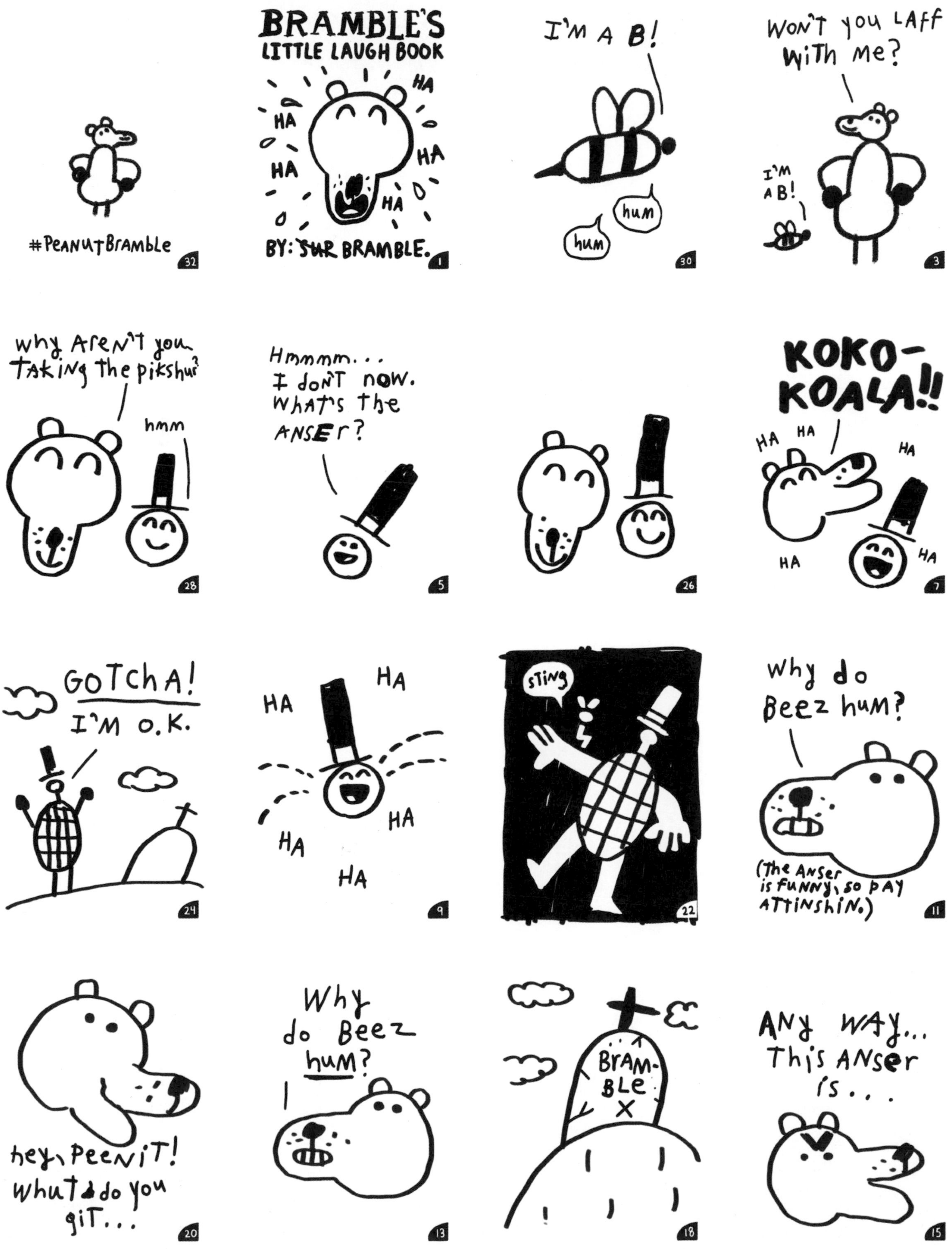

#PeanutBramble
32
BRAMBLE'S
LITTLE LAUGH BOOK
HA
HA
HA
HA
HA
HA
BY: SUR BRAMBLE.
1
I'M A B!
hum
hum
30
WON'T YOU LAFF WITH ME?
I'M A B!
3
why Aren't you taking the pikshur?
hmm
28
Hmmmm... I don't now. What's the ANSEr?
5
26
KOKO-KOALA!!
HA
HA
HA
HA
HA
7
GOTCHA!
I'M O.K.
24
HA
HA
HA
HA
HA
9
STING
22
Why do Beez hum?
(The Anser is funny, so pay attinshin.)
11
hey, peenit! whut do you git...
20
Why do Beez hum?
13
BRAMBLE
18
Any way... This Anser is...
15

NOT ONLY IS IT IMPORTANT FOR READERS TO IDENTIFY WHAT IS HAPPENING IN EACH PANEL, YOUR PANELS CAN ACTUALLY BE PARTS OF OTHER PANELS, ALL CONNECTED TO EACH OTHER! COMICS ARE A GREAT WAY TO USE DIAGRAMS TO COMMUNICATE DETAILED INFORMATION.

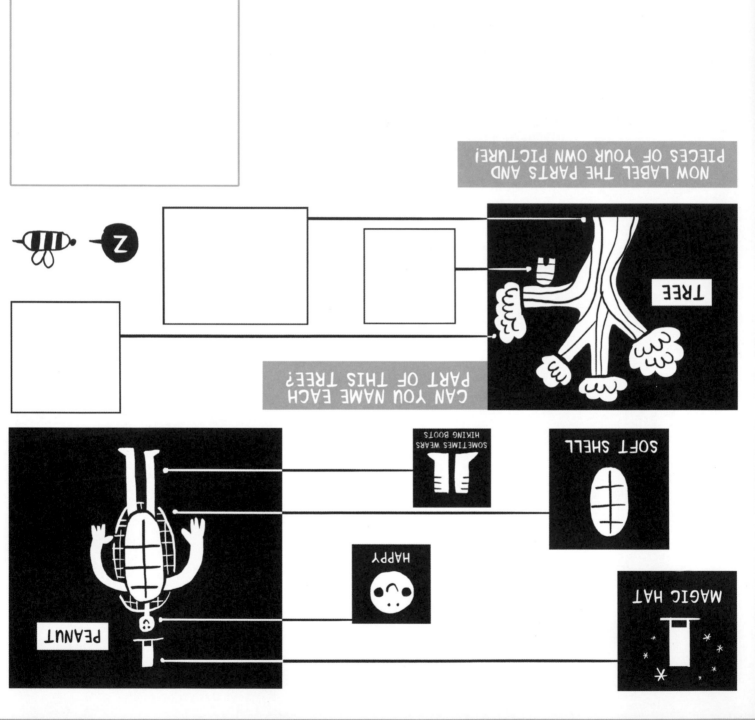

PARTS AND PIECES

I FEEL SO FAR APART!

HAVE YOU EVER LOOKED AT ALL THE PARTS AND PIECES OF A FAVORITE TOY OR A MACHINE, LIKE A CAR OR A COMPUTER? THESE COMICS ARE ALL ABOUT PARTS AND PIECES!

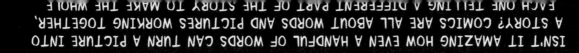

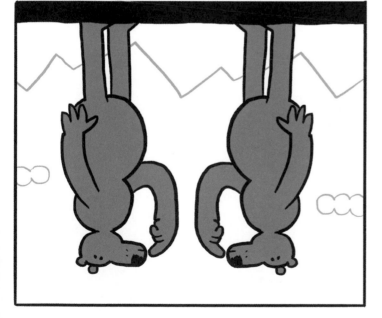

"WOULD YOU LIKE SOME MORE HONEY, BRAMBLE?"

ADD A CAPTION TO EACH OF THE PANELS BELOW. YOU CAN WRITE SOMETHING FUNNY, THOUGHTFUL, OR EVEN SAD--OR SCARY. IT'S UP TO YOU!

CAPTION THIS

END

SHH--I'M READING.
YOU DIDN'T TELL ME
ABOUT THE GIANT
_____ !
(BODY PART)
IT'S SO
GOOD!

ANYWAY, THERE'S THIS
_____
(JOB TITLE)
THAT DISCOVERS A SECRET
_____ ...
(NOUN)
BRAM?
ARE YOU
LISTENING?

BODY PART: _____

NOUN: _____

JOB TITLE: _____

ANY NUMBER: _____

ANIMAL: _____

VERB ENDING
IN "ING": _____

NOUN: _____

ADJECTIVE: _____

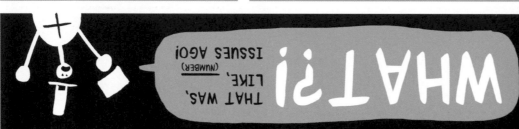

WHAT?!
THAT WAS,
LIKE, _____
(NUMBER)
ISSUES AGO!

HEY, BRAMBLE!
HAVE YOU READ
THE NEW ISSUE OF
_____
(ADJECTIVE)
_____ ?
(NOUN)

IS THAT THE ONE WITH THE
_____
(VERB ENDING IN "ING")
_____ ?
(ANIMAL)

FILL IT IN

ASK A FRIEND TO COME UP WITH ADJECTIVES, NOUNS, AND OTHER WORDS IN
THE LEFT COLUMN, AND THEN USE THE WORDS TO COMPLETE THE COMIC BELOW!

_____ !

GLOSSARY

CAPTION A BOX OR AREA FOR THE NARRATOR'S VOICE, INNER DIALOGUE, OR INFORMATION ABOUT THE CHARACTER OR SETTING.

COLORIST A PERSON WHO COLORS A COMIC.

COMICS WORDS AND PICTURES THAT WORK TOGETHER TO TELL A STORY.

EMANATA LINES AROUND THE HEAD TO INDICATE SHOCK OR SURPRISE.

GUTTER THE SPACE IN BETWEEN PANELS.

INKER A PERSON WHO CREATES THE FINAL INKED DRAWING FOR A COMIC.

INKING USING A BRUSH, PEN, OR MARKER TO CREATE A DRAWING IN INK (TYPICALLY AFTER IT HAS BEEN ROUGHLY DRAWN USING A PENCIL).

PANEL A CONTAINED PART OF THE STORY, OFTEN DRAWN WITHIN A BORDER OR OUTLINE.

PANEL BORDER AN OUTLINE OR BORDER THAT SURROUNDS A PANEL.

PENCILER A PERSON WHO CREATES A ROUGH DRAWING IN PENCIL, BEFORE IT IS INKED.

PENCILING CREATING A ROUGH DRAWING FOR A COMIC, USING A PENCIL.

SCRIPT A DOCUMENT CREATED BY THE WRITER, DESCRIBING THE ACTION, SETTING, AND DIALOGUE OF A COMIC BOOK.

SPEECH BUBBLE A FLOATING SHAPE OR AREA NEAR A CHARACTER'S HEAD, WITH A TAIL LEADING TOWARD THE CHARACTER THAT IS SPEAKING.

UNDERSTANDING COMICS TERMS ALLOWS CREATORS TO IDENTIFY TECHNIQUES AND METHODS, REGARDLESS OF STYLE OR GENRE.

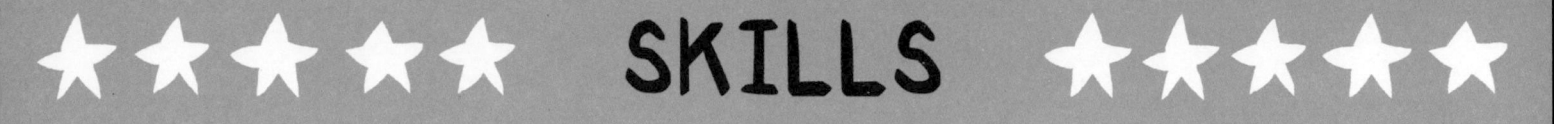

★★★★★ SKILLS ★★★★★

CHARACTER DESIGN

THROUGH GIVING YOUR CHARACTERS ACTIONS TO TAKE, AND BY USING FACIAL EXPRESSIONS AND BODY LANGUAGE IN YOUR PANELS, YOU INVITE THE READER TO PARTICIPATE IN YOUR COMIC.

5, 6, 7, 10, 14, 17, 39

DRAWING

A WELL-WRITTEN COMIC MUST BE ACCOMPANIED BY APPROPRIATELY SKILLED DRAWINGS IN ORDER TO TELL A COMPLETE STORY.

2, 5, 6, 7, 9, 11, 13, 14, 15, 16, 17, 19, 22, 23, 24, 26, 27, 28, 29, 30, 31, 34, 36, 37, 38, 39, 40, 41, 42, 43, 44, 51, 52, 53, 55, 58, 63, 74, 75, 76, 77, 78, 79, 80, 81, 85

FORMATTING

THE SIZE AND SHAPE OF YOUR COMIC WILL HELP DETERMINE THE KIND OF STORY YOU WILL TELL AND WILL HAVE AN IMPACT ON THE READING EXPERIENCE FOR YOUR READERS.

12, 18, 62, 79, 21, 33, 54, 58, 66, 71, 82

IDEA-GENERATING

A CREATOR THAT KNOWS HOW TO COME UP WITH, BUILD, AND FOLLOW-THROUGH ON IDEAS WILL FIND THIS SKILL USEFUL IN EVERY ASPECT OF STORYTELLING THROUGH COMICS.

8, 13, 14, 16, 40, 41, 42, 51, 76, 77, 81

INKING

THE ABILITY TO CREATE CLEAR, EASY-TO-UNDERSTAND ILLUSTRATIONS IN INK WILL HELP YOUR COMIC APPEAR MORE PROFESSIONAL, AND PROVIDE A BETTER READING EXPERIENCE FOR YOUR READER.

11, 18, 19, 22, 24, 25, 28, 41, 52, 53, 57, 56, 63, 72, 74, 75, 77

LETTERING

A GOOD LETTERER KNOWS HOW TO USE STYLE, PLACEMENT, AND DESIGN TO CREATE VISUAL WORDS THAT ADD CHARACTER AND DEPTH TO YOUR ILLUSTRATIONS AND TEXT.

19, 53, 74

PACING

KNOWING WHEN TO "SPEED UP" OR "SLOW DOWN" IN YOUR COMIC WILL MAKE YOUR STORY MORE EXCITING FOR READERS, AND HELP TO FOCUS ON THE MOST IMPORTANT ASPECTS OF YOUR STORY.

6, 12, 15, 18, 62

STORYTELLING

A UNIQUE COMBINATION OF WORDS, PICTURES, CHARACTERS, TONE, AND ACTION WORK TOGETHER TO TELL YOUR STORY. COMICS ARE A SINGULAR FORM OF STORYTELLING, AND CAN DO THINGS THAT EVEN MOVIES AND NOVELS CANNOT.

2, 4, 5, 9, 13, 15, 16, 18, 20, 21, 23, 26, 27, 29, 30, 31, 37, 38, 40, 44, 55, 56, 57, 58, 62, 65, 72, 73, 74, 76, 78, 80, 81, 85, 86, 87

TONE-SETTING

USING MOOD AND ENVIRONMENT AS STORYTELLING TOOLS CAN BE VERY HELPFUL IN CREATING AN EMOTIONALLY CHARGED STORY THAT KEEPS READERS INTERESTED AND EXCITED.

5, 10, 12, 17, 18, 23, 27, 37, 38, 53, 57, 72, 78, 86, 87

VISUAL LITERACY

A GOOD ILLUSTRATION SHOWS THE READER CERTAIN THINGS ABOUT THE CHARACTERS AND ENVIRONMENTS THAT AREN'T MENTIONED OR MADE CLEAR IN THE TEXT.

5, 6, 7, 10, 12, 16, 17, 18, 19, 23, 26, 27, 30, 37, 40, 42, 43, 44, 53, 51, 56, 57, 62, 64, 72, 74, 76, 78, 79, 80, 85

WRITING

A GOOD COMICS WRITER KNOWS HOW TO WRITE A MANUSCRIPT FOR ARTISTS, IDEAS FOR CREATORS AND TEAMS, AND DIALOGUE TO BE USED BY CHARACTERS IN A COMPLETED COMIC.

4, 8, 9, 10, 13, 15, 16, 19, 20, 21, 29, 30, 31, 33, 36, 38, 40, 44, 52, 55, 58, 65, 74, 76, 78, 80, 85, 86, 87

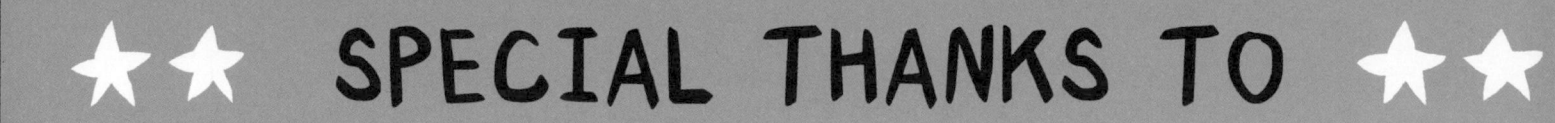

★ ★ SPECIAL THANKS TO ★ ★

ART SPIEGELMAN FOR CREATING ONE OF THE MOST IMPORTANT STORIES IN COMICS AND FOR BEING MY INTRODUCTION TO THE GRAPHIC NOVEL.

CHRIS WARE FOR BEING THE COMICS MEDIUM'S STRONGEST ARGUMENT THAT COMICS ARE LITERATURE.

DOUG TENNAPEL, WHOSE WORK HAS BEEN MY PERMISSION TO PURSUE ALL MY CREATIVE INTERESTS.

QUENTIN BLAKE FOR A LIFETIME OF IMPORTANT WHIMSY THROUGH REWARDING ILLUSTRATIONS AND STORIES.

GHOSTSHRIMP FOR YEARS OF SUPPORT AND ENCOURAGEMENT, AND FOR BEING A POWERHOUSE EXAMPLE TO CREATORS EVERYWHERE.

LYNDA BARRY FOR BEING MY FAVORITE WEIRDO/PROFESSOR IN COMICS.

MIKE MIGNOLA FOR DECADES OF STRANGE AND ENCHANTING STORIES FROM A MASTER STORYTELLER.

LEVI JENSEN, JEREMY ALLEN SILVEIRA, BRAD ASHWORTH, DREW TYNAN ROBBINS, ALEXIS WALKER, AND THE DRAGON'S KEEP CREW FOR YEARS OF FRIENDSHIP AND SUPPORT FOR ME AND OUR LOCAL COMICS COMMUNITY.

PROVO COMIC JAM FOR YEARS OF COMICS EXPLORATION AND FUN.

MITCH PARKER FOR YEARS OF FRIENDSHIP AND AN UNCANNY ABILITY TO MAKE ANYBODY LAUGH.

GENE YANG FOR YEARS OF SUPPORT AND FOR BEING THE PERFECT AMBASSADOR FOR YOUNG PEOPLE'S LITERATURE.

BONNIE KAYE VARGA COOPER FOR SETTING UP MY FIRST COMICS WORKSHOP, WHERE THIS BOOK BEGAN TO TAKE FORM.

JASON, ERIC, JONNIE, AND HIGHER GROUND LEARNING FOR HOSTING YEARS OF COMICS WORKSHOPS, WHERE MANY OF THESE ACTIVITIES WERE BORN.

CARRIE ROGERS WHITEHEAD-GEORGE FOR BEING A RESOURCE FOR READERS, LIBRARIANS, AND EDUCATORS.

JUDY HANSEN FOR USHERING SO MANY GREAT COMICS INTO THE WORLD AND FOR REPRESENTING ME AND MY WORK.

PATRICK BARB FOR HIS KEEN INSIGHT AND EDITORIAL EXPERTISE IN COMPLETING THIS BOOK.

CHLOE RAWLINS FOR HER SHARP EYE AND ARTISTIC PROWESS IN COMPLETING THIS BOOK.

DAN MYERS FOR HIS HELP IN PRODUCTION FOR *LET'S MAKE COMICS!*

LANCE ANDERSON AND JARED ZEMP FOR PLANTING THE SEED OF A WHITE, BLACK, AND BLUE COLOR PALETTE, AND FOR TAKING MY SILLY IDEAS SERIOUSLY.

GEORGE CHEN, WHO ASKED ME TO DRAW A COMIC FOR HIM (WHICH NEEDED A TURTLE AND A BEAR).